Faye Matteson

Smirnoff
for the Soul

ALSO BY YAKOV SMIRNOFF

America On Six Rubles A Day
National Best Seller

YAKOV SMIRNOFF

Smirnoff for the Soul

100 PROOF
Pure Wisdom
Gift Wrapped
in Laughter

Dedication

I dedicate this book to my father, the kindest, funniest and most loving man I have ever met. It was his drive and determination that helped us get out of Russia and come to America.

Our long journey to America began on a cold winter night in Russia, when I was five or six years old. I woke in the middle of the night and heard static coming from the corner of the small room that I shared with my parents. My dad was hunched over with our short-wave radio held tightly to his ear. There was something secretive and forbidden in the intense way he listened. We lived in a tiny apartment with nine other families so Dad had the volume turned down so low that no one else could hear. I was instantly mesmerized.

"Dad, what are you listening to?"

"Shhh," he whispered, "Sit down. I am listening to 'Voice of America.'" He turned the radio towards me so that, with our ears glued to the radio, we could both just barely hear what was being said.

The unclear signal crackled and faded in and out, but through the static I heard a woman's voice say, "Give me your tired, your hungry, your poor." I was thinking, 'I'm qualified.'

My dad tried hard to hang on to the signal. He fiddled with the dial, but the voice vanished into the night.

I said, "Dad, who was that?"

With a dreamy look in his eye, he said, "Son, that was Lady Liberty. She is a stunning woman, standing over 150 feet tall in the middle of a harbor with a torch held high. She waits to greet people who leave their homes, families, friends and everything they own to live in a new country."

I asked my dad why anyone would do that.

He said, "Because the country where Lady Liberty lives is America!"

"In America," he said, "there is enough food for everyone. Families have their own homes with their very own toilets and water inside their house. The people choose their own rulers and they never have to worry about the KGB coming in the middle of the night causing whole families to disappear.

"In America, Yakov, I could be free to invent whatever I can imagine, not just what the government assigns me to work on. I could invent something so magnificent that it will bring joy and comfort to millions of people. If only we could someday go to America!"

I could see how excited my Dad was. I thought, 'what a country this America must be! What a woman Lady Liberty must be! There really must be plenty of food in America to grow women so big. She did sound stunning, except for the green skin!'

I thought to myself, 'I want to meet her! Maybe someday I will!'

That night a dream was born. Dad and I shared a tradition of listening to the 'Voice of America' whenever we could get a signal. Dad warned me that I must tell no one.

One night I fell asleep dreaming of my Lady Liberty. I couldn't wait to get up the next morning. I was so excited. I began to draw her based on what my dad had told me. I drew one picture, then another and then another. When my mom saw what I was doing, she grabbed me. In a frightened voice she said, "Don't let anyone see these pictures! Do you know what will happen to us?"

I was beginning to learn, in Russia, dreams like the one

my dad and I shared could be dangerous. My Dad was a dreamer in his heart. He was an inventor. He invented a lot of neat things. Only a lot of his inventions were just a little off and it used to drive my mother crazy. For example, it was customary to celebrate New Year's by decorating a tree with ornaments and lights. So my dad invented a device that would make our Christmas tree lights blink on and off. Today it's no big deal, but this was back in the 60s. We were the only ones in the Soviet Union with a blinking Christmas tree. It sounds terrific, but unfortunately the device made all the lights in the entire building go on and off... on and off. So on a dark night it looked like our little building was sending secret Morse code messages. My mother yelled at my dad and made him disconnect the blinkin' Christmas tree.

The funny thing was that my dad almost always invented things to try and please my mom. They were just the wrong things. At least, wrong for her. Every time he invented something new he would come to my mom, hoping to win her approval. I was always rooting for my Dad... which was a lot like rooting for the coyote in a road runner cartoon.

Now, I know my mom loved him very much, but she

was a tough critic. She would have made a great Russian ice-skating judge. The most she ever gave him was a 2.9... and then she'd send him off for drug testing.

I grew up and became a professor of art and part-time comedian. As I became more successful as a comedian, my first job was on a Russian cruise ship on the Black Sea. The ship was called the Love Barge, and it was great because it was the first time I met Americans. They were so happy. They were smiling, they had a spark in their eyes. Something I had never seen before. I didn't have to speak the language to know what that spark was. It meant joy, confidence and freedom. You could just tell that these Americans loved their freedom. Like their freedom of speech. We also had freedom of speech in the Soviet Union, but in America you have freedom after you speak...which is a nice little added feature.

Through an interpreter I learned that you had things in America that we didn't have in the Soviet Union ... little things that make a big difference, like the policeman have warning shots. In the Soviet Union, they didn't shoot up in the air, they would shoot you and that would be warning for the next guy.

I spent a lot of time watching Americans, dancing, laughing, taking pictures and just having fun, and always they had that spark in their eyes... I thought it would be great to have that spark in my eyes... and in my parent's eyes... and most of all, I wanted someday to see that spark in my children's eyes.

That's when I made the biggest decision of my life... to try and get out of the Soviet Union and go to America. I couldn't wait to get home and talk to Mom and Dad. I told them I wanted to apply for our visas and we'll all go to America. Right away, my Dad was ready to go. My Mom was ready too. She was ready to kill me for putting another crazy idea in my father's head. My Mom insisted that we drop the subject immediately. But this time my Dad didn't back off. He said, "Klara, let me ask you something. Do you want to see Yakov, twenty years from now, hunched over a tiny radio in the Soviet Union, telling his children about America: a place they can only dream of, or do you want to see Yakov in America, telling his children that they can do and be whatever they dream?"

My mom was silent for a moment, which was itself unusual. Then she said, "You know what happens when you apply for a visa, first you get fired."

"Yes, I know," my dad said.

"Then you have to wait for years to get out. What do

you live on in the meantime if you don't have work? Then what happens if you've been fired and they don't give you the visa? What becomes of you then?"

"I understand," my dad said.

"That's not all," mom continued. "People hear you want to leave, they're afraid to be seen with you. People you think are your friends, they'll cross the street if they see you coming.

"I understand," he said.

"Just so you know. This is what we're going to face."

"What did you say?" my father asked.

"You heard me. This is what we're going to face."

"Let me understand, Klara, how do you feel about going to America?"

My mom said, "Do you think it's actually possible? Even if we got permission, can we afford it?"

That's when my dad gave my mom and me the biggest surprise of our lives. My dad went to the kitchen cupboard and took out a coffee can that was hidden way in the back. Inside, there was money. My mom was shocked. She said, "Where in the world did you get coffee? And where did this money come from?"

Well, it turned out that after all those years of inventing

those crazy gadgets, my dad had actually invented something that was successful. It was a device that measured the integrity of concrete. It was a very big deal because, in the Soviet Union, concrete was the national flower. Of course the communists didn't give him anything near what it was worth, but what they paid him was just barely enough for three airplane tickets to America.

After all those years of people making fun of my Dad's crazy inventions, he didn't want to tell us about the one that really worked, because he wanted to keep the money secret and use it someday to make a better life for us. Well, I must tell you, in my whole life, I had never seen my mom look at my dad with more pride and admiration and love than at that moment. She didn't say anything, she just hugged him, and I could tell that she was holding up a scorecard and on the card was a solid "10."

The next day we all applied for our visas, and the day after that we all got fired. So for two years we lived on whatever my dad could make on his inventions. Then my parents and I finally got permission to leave the Soviet Union. The reason was, Russia desperately needed wheat. The American government said we'll give you wheat if you show some human rights and allow some people out of Russia. So we were traded for two tons of wheat. Now every time I see a Wonder Bread truck, I salute, and then I wonder.

When my parents and I finally got permission to leave the Soviet Union, we knew Dad's inventions and his dreams of coming to America had changed our lives forever.

In September of 2004, I got a call from my mom telling me that Dad was not doing well. Please, come.

Dad's sense of humor was remarkable, even in his last days. He and Mom had managed an apartment building in L.A. for the last fifteen years. Waking up from a two day coma, Dad's first words to my mom were, "Did everybody pay the rent?"

He turned a shopping cart into a make-shift walker that he called his 'chariot.' He used it as he made his last steps on earth.

I had brought two doctor friends with me to L.A. Sleeping on the floor beside my father's bed, they helped keep Dad alive for a few more treasured days, allowing us to have a special conversation.

Dad, although he did not fear death, did have one apprehension about leaving this world. With tears in his eyes, he said, "I can't leave your mother. Who will take care of her? Who will remind her to take her medicine and check the messages on the answering machine? She needs me."

He also shared with me his biggest regret in life. "I patented many inventions in America but none of them became successful. I feel like a failure."

I said, "Dad first of all I will take care of Mom, because you taught me how. Second, about the invention, you do have one that was successful here in America... Me! You created me, taught me how to love, laugh and live the American dream. Without you, I could not have succeeded in America."

Dad smiled and squeezed my hand and his last words were, "I love Klara."

Contents

Get It:
Chasing Happiness Even When It's Running Away from You

Got It:

When Life Points a Finger at You, It's Usually the Middle One

Give It:

"Share the Wealth" Doesn't Mean "Stick 'Em Up"

A Shot of Smirnoff

I was in Times Square and an attractive woman came over to me and asked if I wanted to have a one-night stand for $300. I said, "No, for this kind of money I can buy the whole bedroom set."

Introduction

When I came to America, I didn't have any possessions, but I possessed the power of perception. In the course of my journey to and in America, I learned that love was here for the asking. I was in Time Square and an attractive woman came over to me and asked if I wanted to have a one-night stand for $300. I said, "No!!! For this kind of money, I can buy the whole bedroom set." (I watch *The Price is Right*.) I've also learned the hard way that achieving your dreams isn't the end of the story. When the prince rescued Snow White and they rode off together on his big white horse, the first words out of his mouth could have been, "And just what were you and those dwarfs doing in that house in the woods?"

I remember from my naturalization test that the Declaration of Independence said that all Americans had the right to life, liberty and the pursuit of happiness. For the last 25 years in America, I have discovered that the pursuit of happiness has three stages: Get it, Got it and Give it. You definitely feel those three "G" forces on the roller coasters of life.

First, you want to get it - success, girls, money, girls, houses, girls... you get the drift. You're chasing happiness even when it appears to be running away from you as fast as Willy Nelson running from the IRS. Your focus is on survival, like my family in Russia or like the people on that *Survivor* TV show. After growing up in Russia, I can tell you that the *Survivor* series was shot in the wrong places. They should try the black market in Moscow - now that's survival!

After a while, most people have managed to get enough to feel that they have got it. They have a relationship, kids, a job and 200 channels on satellite TV. They're enjoying their success and their possessions. It's also at this point they can start looking around and asking questions like, "Where the heck am I?" "Why did I think this was so important?" "Is this all there is?" (This question comes up frequently while surfing those 200 TV channels.)

Have you ever watched a kid open a birthday present? Kids are always asking for this toy or that present and they'll swear to you they'll be sooooo happy if you get it for them. But when do they have the most fun? Usually when they're opening the box the present comes in. Once they've opened the gift-wrapped packages they don't care about the toys anymore. They go straight to the "now what?" stage. In a sense we're all just big kids opening presents that we think will make us happy - only to look around and say, "Is that it?"

For me, this happened after I'd been in America for a while and had become a successful comedian. I had the Ferraris, I had the Rolls Royces, I had the house in Los Angeles, I had all the famous friends, but that love and feeling of happiness just wasn't there. That's when fate started pointing a finger at me, the middle one. I learned some painful lessons about what makes people truly happy. This coincided with my move from Los Angeles to Branson, Missouri. In Branson, nobody drives a Ferrari or a Rolls. A guy could be worth a million dollars and he's driving an old beat-up pickup truck. Nobody cares about the externals. They are more interested in who you are as a person. They are also some of the friendliest, most caring people I've ever met.

In this next stage, happiness comes when you give it. The people of Branson helped me discover this next stage in the pursuit of happiness. This is the point where you understand that sharing who you are and what you have with others is what it's all about. It's not just giving material things, but also giving our guidance, time and love to others. Giving brings meaning to life. The soul experiences its fulfillment when it gives and receives, gives and receives in a never-ending flow. This kind of "wealth sharing" will always make you richer because it will give you a much greater life.

Focusing on giving to others is the secret to great comedy as well. Imagine a comedian doing a routine where all he did was crack himself up instead of paying attention to the audience's reactions! (Actually, I've seen comedians like that at an open mic night at the Last Laugh Komedy Klub in Back-of-nowhere, Idaho.)

In my 25 years in America, I've experienced all three stages. I've known a lot of other people who were going through them, too. There's nothing wrong with being in one stage or another, because they're all necessary in the pursuit of happiness. My "pursuit of happiness" has been filled with lessons of love and laughter offered by many amazing souls along the way. I've been blessed with many angels, even though some of them looked more like Jack Nicholson than Della Reese. This book is a collection of stories about the angels of my life and how they've helped me get through the three stages in relatively good shape. Sometimes they helped me by giving me a leg up - often the help looked more like a boot in the bottom, but all along the way, I've been grateful to them for pointing me along the path to true happiness, which isn't dependent on what's outside but really only comes from within.

As a child in Russia, I heard a story about when God was creating the world. He decided he didn't want man to find happiness too easily; he wanted his creations to have to work for it so they would appreciate it more. The fish said, "Let me have it. I can hide it at the bottom of the ocean, they'll never find it there." God answered, "Oh no, I'm creating people to be so clever they will invent machinery and eventually they'll get there." Then the eagle said, "Let me hide it on the top of the mountain. They'll never get there." God replied, "Mankind is persistent. Eventually they'll find a way to climb even the highest mountain." Then God snapped his fingers and said, "I've got it! I'll put it inside of them. That's the last place they'll look."

Many years after I came to America, I read a quote that inspired me: "There are two things to aim at in life. First is to get what you want and after that to enjoy it. Only the wisest of mankind achieve the second." Throughout my time in America, I've enjoyed the time when I was getting it, I enjoyed the time I got it and now, I'm enjoying giving it. I've been fortunate that the life lessons that have helped me get to this place have been gift wrapped in laughter and lifted my spirits. That's why I called this book *Smirnoff for the Soul*.

Get It

Chasing Happiness Even When It's Running Away From You

A Shot of Smirnoff

Nobody can push you around in America, not even a ballet dancer.

Chapter 1

My First Date with Lady Liberty

When I was a little boy in Russia, I saw a picture of the Statue of Liberty. From the moment I laid my eyes on that tall, beautiful woman with the green skin, I fell in love.

Thankfully, my taste in women has changed over the years. I still like them tall but I prefer that they don't oxidize in the elements. From the day I saw Lady Liberty's regal face, I couldn't stop thinking about her. I didn't know that I would spend one of the most important days of my life at her side. Since marrying a statue is illegal in most states, the thought of being sworn in as an American citizen while Lady Liberty looked on was the next best thing.

It was the mid-1980s and there was extensive reconstruction being done on the stately lady I had once admired from afar. Even though I always thought she was perfect, she was getting a face-lift. I learned that once her "nip and tuck" was complete, she would stand witness to a nationally televised swearing-in ceremony for people like myself who were being adopted by the United States. The grand event was scheduled for July 4, 1986, to celebrate her 100th birthday. I pictured myself proudly looking up in her eyes as I held my certificate of citizenship.

Before being approved for citizenship, I was interviewed by an officer of the Immigration and

Naturalization Service. The officer asked me what the Declaration of Independence was and I told him, "How should I know? My whole life I've lived with my parents."

After passing all the tests necessary to become naturalized, I immediately went about trying to get involved in the ceremony on Ellis Island. It turned out to be almost as tough to get on to Ellis Island as it was to get out of Russia.

After making several calls, my excitement was soon dampened by a shower of bureaucracy. As a California resident I was supposed to be naturalized in my home state. I knew there had to be a way to get around that barrier. I couldn't understand how it could be so easy to get sworn at in New York but so difficult to get sworn in there. I wasn't even officially a citizen and I was already trying to use the Constitution to my advantage!

First I researched the idea of having California become part of New York State, but the cost to build a bridge from Lake Tahoe to Buffalo seemed prohibitive, so I reworked my plan of attack. Next, I called everyone I knew in New York and offered to change residences with them. They all felt California was too far to commute to work on a daily basis.

After exhausting all the possibilities I could think of, I

finally accepted what seemed inevitable. I wouldn't be a part of the Statue of Liberty ceremonies. It was extremely disappointing because I had envisioned the occasion so clearly. Even though I was thrilled that I was finally going to become a citizen, I was saddened that somebody else was going to be with my green-skinned girlfriend that day.

After an internal struggle, I finally let it go. If it wasn't meant to be, I wasn't going to force it. As difficult as that was for me, I left it in the hands of fate, knowing that becoming an American citizen was more important than being involved in any special ceremony.

As time passed, I had almost resigned myself to watching the swearing-in ceremony on Ellis Island on TV. Then I received a phone call that would rekindle my flame. The Governor of California at that time, George Deukmejian, called to invite me to represent the State of California at the ceremony. Congress had passed a resolution just five days before the big event allowing two individuals from every state (since I had taken the naturalization test I knew that had to be a hundred people) to be sworn in during the televised ceremony on Ellis Island. I couldn't believe it was happening. I had given up completely on being part of the Statue of Liberty ceremonies and now fate was offering me the best first "American date" I could imagine.

The State of California sent another representative and me to New York, where we joined the other soon-to-be American citizens. We assembled in Battery Park before boarding the ferry to Ellis Island for the ceremony. Immigration officials presented me with a one-foot tall replica of the Statue of Liberty. She immediately became my security blanket. I sat under a tree holding my statue, basking in the glow of this unbelievable day. By this point in my career, I had become a well-known comedian and I signed autographs for a few people who recognized me from television appearances or commercials that I had done.

A little girl saw the others getting autographs and approached. She held out a piece of paper and, as I signed, asked who I was. Joking with her, I told her I was Arnold Schwarzenegger on a diet. She was a beautiful little five year-old who told me that her daddy was becoming a citizen and that he was going to "swear at America". I chuckled and gave her the autograph. As she walked away she waved goodbye, her smile lighting the way.

Although I had made a name for myself as a comedian in America, I was not the most famous Russian at the ceremony that day. In fact, I ran a very distant second to a fellow countryman who was also getting his citizenship, Mikhail Baryshnikov, the ballet dancer who defected from Russia in 1974 during a tour of Canada. He simply walked away from his dance company and never returned to the Soviet Union.

Baryshnikov arrived surrounded by a handful of FBI agents. The media was buzzing, but the FBI wouldn't let them near him. I hoped Baryshnikov wouldn't sit next to me, just in case a KGB sniper might want to knock off two Russian birds that flew the coop with one shot.

Since this was a democracy, we drew numbers to determine seating before the ceremony began. I didn't fare too well and drew 98 out of 100. I took my place in the last row, which was so far back it had a New Jersey zip code. Even though I wasn't up front, believe me, I was delighted to be anywhere on Ellis Island.

I sat down and only had time to pinch myself and take several appreciative breaths when a stranger approached.

He was a handsome Arab who thrust his big, callused hand toward me. He had a vise-like grip and he shook my hand vigorously. To my surprise, the man told me he had a seat up front that he would like me to have.

I was stunned. "Why?" I asked.

He said, "You were nice and signed an autograph for my daughter. It's my way of saying thank you, Mr. Schwarzenegger." He winked at me and I'm pretty sure he knew I wasn't really Arnold, but he was grateful that I had made his little girl smile.

He insisted that I take his spot and I didn't want to argue with him, just in case he decided to shake my hand again. I thanked him profusely and stepped quickly to the front where I sat in my new seat, clutching my statue the same way I had held my luggage the day I left Russia. This was fast becoming the best day of my life.

A Pakistani gentleman was sitting next to me, smiling like George W. Bush at a Texas barbecue. Suddenly, the FBI agent approached him and demanded he give up his seat because they wanted Baryshnikov to sit in the front row. When the great dancer arrived, they made the Pakistani gentleman move to the back.

The ceremony was about to begin and a producer called

out, “One minute to live broadcast!” Just then, the Pakistani man returned. He stood over Baryshnikov, holding his ticket in his hand. He stared down at the much smaller dancer and in broken English said, “This is America and that’s my seat.” The FBI agents were so shocked they almost let an expression slip onto their faces. To his credit, Baryshnikov actually got up, nodded in understanding and went to a seat near the back. It was the first time I had actually seen an ordinary citizen stand-up to the authorities without being whisked away. The Pakistani man sat down beside me and a big smile returned to his face. I instantly realized why I had worked so hard to come to this country in the first place. Nobody can push you around in America, not even a ballet dancer.

We were going to be sworn in by Chief Justice Warren Burger. 'Burger, what a great American name,' I thought. The Chief Justice began with the phrase, “My fellow Americans.” I was so excited because I realized that he was talking to me! The first thought that went through my mind as an American was, “What are all of these foreigners doing in my country?”

My swearing-in ceremony fulfilled the dream I had for

so many years - to become an American. I sat quietly in the corner admiring my statue, clutching my citizenship papers and relishing the moment. I realized that I had learned two huge lessons. First, to have things happen in your life you need to have intention, put your attention on your intention and have no tension about your intention. Second, you can go to Italy but you cannot become an Italian citizen, you can go to France but you cannot become a Frenchman, but you can come to America and become an American.

A Shot of Smirnoff

My dad was happy that his chemistry experiment hadn't turned his Russian son into Swiss cheese. He wouldn't have lost a son; he would have lost his life, because mother would have killed him.

Chapter 2

Go With Your Gut (And I Don't Mean to the "All-You-Can-Eat" Buffet)

Leaving Russia was not easy, to say the least, but I trusted my "gut feeling" that I wanted to go to America, so my parents and I left the hammer and sickle behind for the stars and stripes. It turned out to be the best decision of our lives. A gut feeling is more than just a queasy belly after downing a plate of nachos and then riding the tilt-a-whirl. When you're on a date, for example, and the girl leaves for the bathroom at 6:00 and never comes back, your gut instinct tells you that it might be going badly. I believe that when life throws a difficult situation your way, that gut feeling is your soul guiding you to make the right decision. My dad helped me learn the lesson that there is something within each of us that knows what to do in a split second and can stimulate us to react in time to do the right thing - without thought and without doubt.

My father was a frustrated inventor. I remember him puttering around the house on various projects when I was a little kid. Even though we often didn't have enough food to sustain a rodent of any kind, my father was always trying to build a better mousetrap. In fact, we had so few crumbs that mice used our apartment for survival training. Dad had a special skill for making luxuries from common items he found around the house. He made McGyver look like a novice.

On the day of my 8th birthday, my dad told me about balloons that could float in the air. (Of course, we had balloons in Russia, they just didn't float. There was an old joke about even the balloons being depressed by communism.) My dad called these special balloons "happy balloons" and promised to make me one. He didn't know how to do it at the time, but he knew he could figure it out.

So he put on his thinking cap and then did extensive research, which in Russia meant talking to the neighbors. He found out that if he put battery acid in a bottle and added zinc, the byproduct would be helium. Since helium was lighter than air, the result would be homemade happy balloons. I didn't really know what zinc or acid was, but the idea of a happy balloon got me pretty excited.

What happened next remains vivid in my memory. There I was, standing patiently in the living room (which was our makeshift laboratory), wearing my new birthday outfit, helping my dad make me a happy balloon. Now, in Russia you didn't get new clothes too often, so I was very proud of that outfit - proud as Adam in his birthday suit.

Since my father didn't really know how much acid and zinc to combine, he did what most "kitchen" scientists do, he made an uneducated guess. He filled an old soda bottle with acid and planned to throw some zinc in and cover the mouth of the bottle with a balloon. The chemical reaction would then fill the balloon with helium and voila! A happy balloon.

My job was to hold the balloon over the mouth of the bottle after my dad put in the zinc. However, it was quickly apparent that zinc and acid don't like each other (kind of like Republicans and Democrats). The contents of the bottle began bubbling vigorously, quickly climbing up the neck of the bottle. Before I had a chance to slip the end of the balloon over the bottle, a volcanic eruption of putrid white froth began to flow freely out of the neck and over my bare hand. My dad sprang into action. He tried to protect me by grabbing the bottle and pressing his thumb over the top to prevent the contents from spilling over.

If you've ever been to a frat party where some joker shakes up a bottle full of beer, you know what happened next. My dad's strategy caused pressure to build inside the bottle. It quickly surpassed the ability of his thumb to contain it. Suddenly a spray of acid seltzer erupted from the bottle. My dad turned his face away and did his best to protect me, but some of the acid got on me. I felt like a bathtub under attack by a shower of the meanest scrubbing bubbles ever. I screamed and my dad turned to see what was happening. Instinctively he grabbed the closest thing to him, a box of baking soda. He ripped open the top and in one swift motion threw it on me. (Looking back, I'm glad the closest thing to my father wasn't a box of corn flakes.)

The powder covered me from head to toe. I looked like I belonged on an episode of *I Love Lucy*. While my father began brushing me off, I stood there thinking about putting myself up for adoption. The baking soda had done something miraculous. It neutralized the acid. My dad checked my whole body, but I didn't have a single burn. However, my birthday outfit didn't fare so well. It was covered with specks, which at first we assumed were powder. They didn't brush off because they weren't specks, they were hundreds of tiny holes. My new outfit had been turned into cheesecloth.

I didn't care. I was just glad the holes were in my birthday outfit, not my "birthday suit." I could have become a "holey" boy, but instead my clothes had protected me. My dad was happy, too - happy that his chemistry experiment hadn't turned his Russian son into Swiss cheese. He wouldn't have just lost a son, he would have lost his life because my mother would have killed him.

We both stood in our apartment, my dad breathing a huge sigh of relief, me still clutching the balloon, wearing a shirt full of holes and a big smile. My dad and I learned a valuable lesson that day - don't let the neighbors teach you chemistry. I learned something even more important though. I learned about listening to the little voice inside. There was a source of instinctive wisdom inside my dad that directed his actions. He told me later that he didn't know the baking soda would help. He just grabbed it and threw. Where did that instinct come from? If he had tried to figure out the best reaction with his conscious mind, my life might be totally different today. I might still be on stage, but at country fairs as a freak show.

I'm glad my dad listened to that internal voice and acted on what he heard. It was a little miracle and a gift far more important than a happy balloon. The memory has often helped to remind me that the soul always knows what to do. I do my best to listen to that little voice whenever I'm faced with any kind of difficult situation. Sometimes that little voice leads me to one too many trips to the all-you-can-eat buffet at "Troughs-a-Plenty," but for the most part my gut keeps me out of trouble.

A Shot of Smirnoff

My mom didn't really like animals. I guess she figured she was already looking after two of us.

Chapter 3

Don't Judge a Bird by its Feathers, or a Hedgehog by Its Needles

Looking back, I guess one of my favorite activities when I was younger was going to the open market with my father. It was a place where people could exchange food, goods and animals. It was complete with seedy pitchmen who looked like they had been released from jail for two days and were getting ready to go back. We always went to see the animals. If it's one thing my dad and I shared, it was the love of animals. My mom didn't really like them - I guess she figured she was already looking after the two of us, so why add any more animals to the list? In truth, my mom was scared of most animals, and she really hated mice. She was the only one I've ever seen who ran screaming from the movie *Stuart Little* as soon as the talking mouse showed up.

My dad and I used to go to the open market every week, even though the animals didn't change that often. It was just great spending quality time with my dad. I got my first pet at the open market - a hedgehog. It's kind of like a porcupine, but with shorter needles. I named him Pokey. He stayed in the closet and protected our stuff from burglars. However, petting Pokey was a pain, literally. I quickly learned that after you pet a hedgehog, everything else is soft and cuddly.

The one story that sticks out in my mind is about a bird I wanted. I had many birds over the years because they stayed in cages and we didn't have much room. (The hedgehog in the closet had more room than we did.) One day my dad and I were at the market looking around, pretty much just hanging out together, when I saw a group of birds in this one cage. All the birds were very lively, except for one droopy bird that just sat in the corner. He didn't chirp or anything.

I asked the man what was wrong with that bird. I thought maybe he was a nerd bird and nobody liked him because he had zits on his beak or something. The guy told me he was a sick bird and he probably wouldn't make it through the night. The bird needed medicine that wasn't available and he kept trying to sell me another bird.

I don't know what drew me to that bird. Maybe it reminded me of how I felt in school when nobody wanted to talk to me. I pleaded with my dad to buy me the bird and told him that maybe it just needed love. My dad backed me up and got me the bird. The guy didn't even charge us. He said we were saving him the time it would take to bury it. We took the bird and headed home. I was so happy and I immediately named the bird Lucky.

As soon as dad and I got home, we gave the bird water

and food, along with a clean cage hung right by the window. Before I went to bed that night, I prayed that the bird would still be alive when I woke up. It seemed like it took me forever to fall asleep after I put the sheet over the cage. I finally managed to doze off only to be awakened, what seemed like a minute later, by the sound of Lucky chirping. He was as good as new. It seems that love sometimes works better than any medicine.

Lucky turned out to be our best bird ever. He would fly around the room all day and then, promptly at 6:00, he would fly right back into his cage. Lucky taught me a valuable lesson about life: You can't judge a book by its cover and you can't judge a bird by its feathers. You have to give a bird, or a person, a chance to fly around and prove what he's made of. When I went to America, I too, felt "Lucky." Like my bird, when I came to this country, I felt as if I had been given water, food, sunshine and love. Because of that, I was able to spread my wings and fly.

A Shot of Smirnoff

Freedom is like Chinese food; once you have a taste of it, you'll always be hungry for more.

Chapter 4

You Are Special - Just Like Everybody Else

I've learned that happiness comes in many ways but always includes one vital ingredient: Appreciation. It is often overlooked completely and seldom considered important. So much of our activities revolve around what people call the almighty dollar. You'd almost think it had God's picture on it instead of George Washington's, but many studies have revealed that people who feel appreciated are much more likely to remain loyal in their jobs.

In Russia we were raised to cherish the flag and all it stood for. However, the Soviet flag was the only one in the world with tools on it. I think honoring your country is basically a good idea, but the Russian system had one fatal flaw: We were supposed to live by the motto, "One for all and all for one." The "all for one" part never really worked its way back to the people it was supposed to, though. In reality, the people were just cogs in a giant machine. We were considered exactly the same as each other - replaceable, expendable parts. If we couldn't do our jobs we'd be replaced, just like shark's teeth (I saw that on the Discovery Channel).

On one occasion, I was scheduled to work the Russian Cruise Line. No, that's not a joke, there were several very luxurious cruise ships that sailed the Black Sea. Of course, the passengers were upper-class Russian and foreign tourists. The only lower-class Russians on board were, what else, working staff. The ship I was scheduled to perform on was called the Love Barge. That's what I called it, anyway.

Since I was receiving next-to-nothing in pay, I phoned to ask if my parents could have a cabin on the ship. The entertainment director laughed at me. "This is Russia," he said. "Who do you think you are, Wayne Newton? No extra privileges and no cabin."

I was very disappointed, so I responded by threatening to cancel the engagement. "Fine," the entertainment director said, "We'll just get someone else," and we hung up. If you think fighting with the American government is hard, try fighting with the Kremlin. It makes a boxing match with Mike Tyson look like a high school prom.

Later that afternoon, however, I got a big surprise. A messenger arrived with my tickets for the cruise. I mean, our tickets - my parents' and mine. I couldn't believe it. All my life I had only known the supremacy of the state. If the government said no to you, it was over. I was thrilled because I had never beaten the government before. I felt like Sylvester Stallone in the *Rocky* movie, only with a lot fewer muscles, less sweat and better diction.

A few days later, we boarded the ship. My parents went to their cabin and I went to mine. My parents and I still shared a one-room apartment in Odessa, Russia. I think all three of us thought we had died and gone to heaven instead of boarding a ship. We were immediately informed that we were scheduled to have dinner with the captain of the ship that evening. My parents were acting like teenagers on prom night when their chaperone passes out. They kept saying "Jacuzzi" over and over. A Russian Jacuzzi is very different than an American one. In Russia, it's a bathtub and a big box of Alka-Seltzer.

We got dressed up and went to dinner with the captain, where we received the full four-star treatment (which is like one-star treatment in America - the exchange rate, you know). I asked the captain how it happened that my parents and I were being treated so well. He said, "Yakov, I saw you onstage and I wanted you on my ship. I believe you're not just another comedian. You've got something special."

I confessed to him that I was surprised at his power. "Russian cruise ships are sometimes chartered by American companies," he told me. "I've learned from those trips that in America people with special skills receive special acknowledgment. There, the more skilled you are, the more you are rewarded, because America appreciates its people."

I knew about those special charter cruises. I had seen

other Russian crew members come back from such cruises. It was like watching Cinderella coming back from the ball. They had new clothes on, the women wore make-up and they had seen movies that no one in Russia would be allowed to watch. More important, they had been exposed to a whole new world of people who appreciated their talents and rewarded them accordingly. Because I didn't speak English, however and I was so popular in front of the Russian audience, the authorities would never let me go on those American cruises. Maybe, if I had, I never would have left Russia, but I doubt it. Freedom's like Chinese food, once you have a taste of it, you're always hungry for more.

I did my show on that ship all week, a week that will always be etched in my memory. Not for the food, the Jacuzzi, or anything else about the cruise itself, but for my first taste of capitalism. It remains sweet to this day. Later, when I became a well-known comedian in America and was able to buy things, I realized that I wasn't doing comedy for the money, but for the respect and appreciation that I received every time I walked out onstage. That's what capitalism means to me, the opportunity to capitalize on your skills through the magic medium of appreciation.

No matter what you do or where you work, everyone has a deep need to be appreciated. All leaders have known that or they soon have no one left to lead. We found that out in Russia. Communism looked good on paper, but in reality it wasn't enough to be an equal part of a supposedly fair but heartless system. What we needed was more than physical. Our souls needed appreciation. We needed to be awarded for being special, not equal.

If you write a letter to Russia, you have to put the address on the envelope in this order: the name of the country, then the name of the state, then the name city, then the street and then the person's name comes last. I am proud and happy to now live in a country where people always come first.

A Shot of Smirnoff

Some friends and family considered us traitors. They treated us like AT&T employees who had MCI service at home.

Chapter 5

Pay No Attention to the Man Behind the (Iron) Curtain

My journey from communist Russia to the United States was filled with obstacles. As you can imagine, the decision to immigrate from Russia to America wasn't easy for my parents and me. My dream of becoming a successful entertainer in America gave me the strength to forge ahead in spite of the setbacks and challenges.

The only important things we were leaving behind were our friends and family. It wasn't until we actually got to Customs and Immigration on my last day in Russia that I realized how essential it was to give up a little in order to gain a lot.

Contrary to popular belief, it was possible to get out of Russia during the communist era without bribing a KGB officer with such gems as two-ply Charmin or Spam. Even though my parents were both around 60 and I had lived the first 26 years of my life in the Soviet Union, we applied to the government to immigrate to America. Now, Americans may think of this move as a "no-brainer," after all, why would we want to stay in Russia, right?

Well, most Russians didn't see it that way. Imagine how you would feel if one of your relatives or friends decided to leave the great democracy of the United States and move to some vast foreign land where people talk a different language, wear funny hats and live by a totally different set of rules - someplace like Texas!

The first thing that happens in Russia when you apply for immigration is that you get fired from your job. Believe me, they don't give you a gold watch when you leave. Being out of work for a few weeks while you're getting ready to immigrate might not sound so bad, but there was no unemployment insurance in the Soviet Union and it wasn't like you could just open up a Domino's franchise and start delivering pizza to the Kremlin. Financially it was tough, but emotionally it was worse. Some friends and family considered us traitors. They treated us like AT&T employees who had MCI long distance service at home.

We waited a long time for everything in Russia, including getting out of Russia. Our few weeks turned into two and a half years of scraping by. I'm not sure what criteria the government used to decide who was allowed to leave and who was forced to stay, but I can picture several communist bureaucrats playing "Red Rover, Red Rover, send Yakov on over."

There we stood in our scantily furnished one-room apartment while my father read the letter notifying us we had been approved to leave. I stared at my parents and a sense of uncertainty hit me. My mother was understandably nervous. "How can we bear to leave all of this?" she said, pointing to the four or five pieces of furniture and a collection of mismatched dishes. When my father and I finally stopped laughing we began packing our bags for the most important journey of our lives.

Government regulations were very specific on what we were allowed to take out of the country: one hat, one camera, one coat, two pairs of pants and two shirts, in other words, most of what you owned. The next day we said our good-byes to the few friends and relatives who had stood by us through that tumultuous time and we left for the train station.

We stood in line for over ten hours waiting for customs officials to interview us one last time. As we waited for our turn, I became increasingly anxious. I had heard horror stories about others who were just steps away from boarding the train to freedom only to be grabbed at the last moment and whisked away to who-knows-where. We understood how important it was to maintain our composure. By the way, who-knows-where is in Siberia, just north of how long-is-my-sentence and east of I-shouldn't-have-told-the-KGB-to-mind-their-own-business.

The train whistle sounded, signaling five minutes until departure. We reached the front of the line and were ordered to open our suitcases. The customs officer stared at me with his tiny, angry eyes that were almost hidden by his fat wrinkled head. He looked like one of those dolls made from dried-up apples that you find in country stores - without the cute red and white checked dress, that is.

He rifled through our suitcases with his meaty hands and held up my father's watch. I couldn't believe it when he put it on his own wrist. He attempted a joke by saying something like, "It's about time I got a new watch." My father remained stoic and I tried desperately to stifle my anger. The officer went on to steal my mother's favorite necklace and began examining a camera my mother had given to me for my 10th birthday. He held it up and said, "This will make a fine gift for my son". He placed the camera back in its case and stuffed it inside his coat pocket. I cherished that camera and I tried to hide the pain in my eyes from the customs officer.

The longest few seconds of my life began to tick away as the officer eagerly waited for my reaction. I wanted to jump across the table and squeeze the juice out of that dried-apple face of his but I knew I'd end up mining zinc in I-should-have-kept-my-mouth-shut. I clenched my teeth and balled up my fist when I felt my father gently squeezing my arm. “Remember the monkeys,” he whispered.

At first I thought my father had gotten into the celebratory vodka a little early, but I remembered something he had told me years before. He said, “When the tribesmen in Africa wanted to capture monkeys, they would hollow out a coconut, secure it to the ground and fill it full of rice. The hole was big enough for the monkey to get his hand in, but when he made a fist around the rice he couldn’t get his hand out. If the monkey wanted to be free, he had to drop the rice, but the monkeys never did.”

I’m here today because my dad was a wise man. I relaxed my fist and managed to smile at the thickheaded officer. I said to him in a polite but somewhat subversive tone, “I hope you enjoy our things.” The embarrassed civil servant couldn’t look me in the eye any longer. He threw my camera back in the suitcase, closed our bags and impatiently waved us through.

When we reached the platform, the train was crawling away from the station and beginning to pick up speed. I could barely keep up with my elderly parents who were running faster than a speeding... well, faster than I was. I finally caught up with them and we heaved our suitcases onto the stairs of the train and climbed up. After we caught our breath, we hugged each other and danced a little jig. We were actually getting out of Russia! We may have lost most of our material possessions that day, but we gained something that couldn't fit in any suitcase - our freedom.

Years later, I told my mother that I wanted to return to Russia for a visit. She said there was someone she wanted me to see. I asked, "Who, my aunt in Moscow?" She said, "No, a psychiatrist in Los Angeles. You must be crazy to want to go back there!"

A Shot of Smirnoff

The flavor of my drinks improved dramatically when Nick explained what "on the rocks" really meant.

Chapter 6

The "Spirits" of Christmas Past

My parents and I arrived in America on a blustery New York day just a few weeks before Christmas. We had very little money so my parents were worried that we wouldn't be able to celebrate our first American Christmas properly. Even though they were concerned, I remained calm because I had a plan. I decided to become a bartender. You see, in Russia it's an easy job. There are only three drinks: vodka, two glasses of vodka and a bottle. I took almost all of the money I'd saved in Russia and paid my tuition for a School of Mixology (a division of Cocktail Academy). I would earn a prestigious degree in bartending, earn money-pouring drinks and then surprise my parents with a Christmas feast to remember. I decided bartending would be the perfect job because I wanted to meet Americans, learn their language and - in the case of American women - learn their phone numbers. After a few days of bartending, I realized the only time you use most of those words you learn in a bar are when you're in a New York taxi or when you slam your fingers in the door.

One problem: my English wasn't very good and I couldn't understand the teacher. I didn't realize this would be perfect training for dealing with the speech patterns of bar patrons. Being the clever fellow that I am, I took a tape recorder to class. I recorded the teacher's lectures and then listened to them at home. I don't know why I thought I would understand his English better at home than in class. I tried to practice making drinks at home, too. Mixing drinks there was tricky, though, since all we had was tap water and olives.

I really had no idea what I was doing. I graduated two weeks later a certified Mixologist. That claim to fame didn't get me nearly as many dates as the brochure said it would. When I tried to tell the teacher I didn't feel that I had learned enough about bartending and I needed extra training, he told me not to worry because the customers would be drunk. So there I was, a bartending certificate in one hand and a tuition bill that made me want to start drinking in the other.

Fortunately for me (and not so fortunate for the patrons), I got a bartending job a couple of days later at the Monk's Inn Restaurant in Lincoln Center. They provided me with a sack-like burlap uniform which looked like a UPS package you'd ship a monk in, hence the name of the restaurant. I'm grateful they didn't make me get the haircut.

Since my English was so bad, the thought of being a monk in my first job in America was appealing. I thought I could hide my deficiency by taking the vow of silence. However, my fears about speaking English subsided when I arrived on the job and met the waiters. Some of them were from Czechoslovakia and Yugoslavia and they spoke a little Russian. They were friendly to me considering some of them were in America only because Russians had forcibly taken over their countries. I started to relax and feel more confident.

At 5:00 P.M. the customers started pouring in - my cue to start pouring. Unfortunately, by then I had forgotten how to make everything except a Scotch and water. I could only make that if a customer pointed behind me, showing where the Scotch was.

To hide the fact that I had no idea what I was doing, I kidded around with the customers. One guy asked me if Yakov Smirnoff was my real name and I told him "No, it's Jack Daniels." A lady asked me for a very, very dry Martini, so I gave her an empty glass with an olive in it and said, "That's as dry as they come."

People quickly grew impatient with me. One guy said, "You don't know what a screwdriver is, do you? It's the easiest drink in the world - vodka and orange juice. Now make me one and don't ever forget it!" I felt bad that he yelled at me, so I improvised and made him my own version: vodka, orange juice and milk of magnesia. I called it a "Phillip's Screwdriver." I don't think he will ever forget it.

Nobody else was appreciating my jokes and, with my English, they probably didn't understand them either. The customers were mad, the waiters were mad and the shift manager was hotter than McDonald's coffee. By 6:00 P.M. the waiters were jumping over the bar to make their own drinks and yelling at me in a variety of languages, all of which seemed to share the same four-letter words (and I don't mean "love"). It was like having the entire United Nations mad at you. Defeated, I slumped on the floor in a corner and wondered what the fastest way back to Russia would be. At least there I would only be cursed at in one language.

Even before the shift ended, the manager, Bob, shouted, "We don't need you here!" I didn't understand whether this meant I had lost the job or that my shift was over. The reality was that I had been fired from my very first job. I was broke and without work, closer to being an actual monk than I ever wanted to be. I sat on the steps outside the restaurant and watched my tears fall to the pavement. It was the night before Christmas and even Yakov was not stirring. I had just spent most of my life savings to learn how to be a bartender. I felt bad about being fired and even worse knowing my parents were expecting me to buy food for our first holiday feast in America. The chances were the only turkey at the table would be me.

Just when I was ready to walk home to tell my parents the bad news, I felt a hand on my shoulder. Great, I thought. First I get fired, now I'm getting mugged. I looked up and saw Nick, the night bar manager. Nick was from Czechoslovakia and he spoke to me in Russian. He asked me why I was upset and I told him what had happened.

"Yakov, you've got a lot to learn about being an American," Nick said. "Now, I won't lie to you, you're probably the worst bartender I've ever seen. I heard a customer asked you for a seven and seven and you told him it was fourteen." At that point I was hoping he'd start to bend the truth and save my feelings, but he continued. "You don't get it yet, but listen, don't give up. In this country we keep practicing until we get better. Just look at our politicians: they haven't got a clue what they're doing, but do you see them giving up?"

Nick held out his hand and helped me to my feet. He looked me square in the eye and I'll never forget what he said to me. "Yakov, you're a good man and you can be good at anything you want to be, but right now you need to be a good bartender. Let's go back inside and I'm going to work with you all night if I have to."

"But it's too late," I exclaimed, "I'm already fired."

Nick shook his head, and then smiled. "Yakov, it's Christmas, I'll talk Bob into bringing you back. Come on!"

Despite his urging I was too ashamed to return and face everyone. Nick got frustrated with me. "Listen Yakov, you've got to get over it," he said.

I didn't understand the phrase. Then again, there were lots of American phrases I didn't understand, like "Learn to play guitar - no strings attached." I asked, "What do you mean, 'get over it?'"

"Right now you're feeling sorry for yourself," he replied. "I know this must seem overwhelming, but you're bigger than this problem. You always are, no matter how big a problem might seem. You've done it in your life - it's like getting over the Berlin wall. It means getting it and being able to see opportunity on the other side. Now, come on!"

I followed Nick back inside. With his help I began to remember what I had learned in school. As we "stirred the spirits" I felt my own spirits begin to rise and gradually got the hang of things. For instance, I learned right away that you don't put tequila in a white wine spritzer. The flavor of my drinks improved dramatically when Nick explained what "on the rocks" really meant.

When my shift began I was nervous. Now, with Nick's encouragement and faith in me I began to feel confident. I finished the shift without getting fired again and then stayed until 4:00 A.M. testing new drinks on myself. Nick called this "method bartending." By the end of the night I was feeling much better, I'll tell you. This was turning into a drunken version of *It's a Wonderful Life*. When they invited me to come back to work the next day I was overjoyed. I asked Nick, "Why are you helping me?" He said, "Because I have a son in Czechoslovakia and I just hope someone is helping him."

On my way home I felt like the king of the world, just like Leonardo DiCaprio without the iceberg. If I could do this, I could do anything here! I stopped to buy food for our first Christmas holiday feast in America and it was one of the most special meals my family and I ever shared.

I only worked at the Monk's Inn for one week before I got an offer to work at Grossinger's Hotel in the resort area of the nearby Catskill Mountains. Although it would be tough to give up that potato sack uniform, I knew this was a real break because I would be working near the big comedy and music shows. I felt guilty about deserting Nick after he had been so kind to me, but I told him about the job and he said, "Listen Yakov, never turn down an opportunity."

"But I don't want to leave you shorthanded," I countered.

He smiled and said, "Don't worry, I'll get over it."

We shook hands and I left for my next job in America, knowing that I would not forget this stranger who had taught me to never give up. As I walked out the door he yelled, "Yakov, if you ever need a job, you have one here."

As I walked home that night, I realized something that stopped me in my tracks. The name "Nick" is short for "Nicholas"... I had met a real Saint Nicholas. Even better, this St. Nick didn't have a cheap cotton beard, bad breath or try to make me sit on his lap. Nick had helped turn my family's first Christmas in America from a nightmare into a dream come true.

I've lived in America for over twenty years now and I know that Nick was just one of millions of people who play Santa every day for others in need. They serve meals at soup kitchens for the homeless. They help their neighbor's daughter find her lost cat. They deliver Christmas presents to families who can't even afford their own tree. The lesson I learned from Nick was the real meaning of the phrase "get over it." It doesn't mean forget about it and move on. It means you have to rise above the problem to find the solution on the other side.

As Evil Knievel told his son when the kid started riding motorcycles, the most important thing you can do is get over it.

A Shot of Smirnoff

"I'm Yakov from Russia," I said. "So where do Russians hang out in Texas?" He said, "On a tree, boy."

Chapter 7

Just Like Peanut Butter, Real Friends Stick With You

In 408 B.C., Euripides wrote that friends show their love more in times of trouble than in happiness. I'm not big on history - it's a subject that gets older every year, but this saying reminded me of how I met the man who turned out to be my best friend, Gary Powell.

Phil Manus, the manager of the bar at Grossinger's Resort, where I had been working, moved to Miami and told me to look him up if I ever hit town. Things had gotten very slow at Grossinger's, so I decided to take Phil up on his offer. I drove down to Miami, got an apartment and started working for Phil (I may have been the first person from a communist country to arrive in Miami not on a raft). Before I left New York, however, I had sent out resumes to several cruise ship companies. I'd been a successful entertainer on Russian cruise ships, so I figured, how different could American cruise ships be?

One day the phone rang. It was my parents calling from New York, telling me that the Royal Caribbean cruise line had called. They needed an assistant cruise director for a ship that was sailing from Miami! I would be paid $200 a week in cash plus room and board. That was a lot of money to me at the time. I could send money to my parents and perhaps have a little left over. It was closer to show business than standing behind a bar listening to drunken customers making bad jokes about my name.

I told Phil about the job offer and he said, "Yakov, I

know this your dream. Go for it." I arrived at the pier about an hour before the ship left port, suitcase in hand. We set sail without my ever being interviewed for the job I was supposed to fill. In Russia there was a cruise director aboard the ship, but he was more of an administrator, like a hotel manager. I thought perhaps an American cruise director was more like a movie director. Maybe when the ship was doing something the cruise director didn't like, the assistant cruise director would yell, "Cut!" However, I soon found out exactly what was expected of an American cruise director and English was one very important requirement. Oops - I hadn't mentioned on my application that my English was still at the "See Jane run. See Spot hide. Hide, Spot, hide" level.

The cruise director gave me some thorough training. Unfortunately, it was all in English and I understood only about 30 percent of what he had said. Even with the language problems, I couldn't have been happier. The ship's staff were the ones who performed in the talent show, so every person on staff had to have some sort of talent. I would be able to tell a couple of jokes and do a Russian dance. If you looked at it the right way (sideways), I was one step closer to being a professional entertainer in America. Of course, I didn't realize at the time that I was doomed to fail, kind of like an Enron executive taking a lie detector test.

After my first day at sea I was already in way over my head with my co-workers. In fact, if it had been a pirate ship they probably would have had me walk the plank somewhere off the coast of St. Thomas. The staff was trained to look happy, but when they'd see me suddenly it was "Frown City." I began to feel less than appreciated and welcomed.

That same day, however, I met a gentleman from Texas (yes, I know, it's hard to believe there are gentlemen in Texas, but there are). Gary Powell was an assistant cruise director just like me - only he was 6'3" with blond hair and a cowboy hat. The first night on board, I was sitting with the rest of the staff having dinner and he introduced himself. He said, "Hi, I'm Gary Powell. I'm from Texas."

"I'm Yakov, from Russia," I said. "So, where do Russians hang out in Texas?"

"On that thar tree, boy, " Gary answered, with a steely-eyed glare that would have done Clint Eastwood proud.

Everybody laughed and I thought, Oops, he's going to be a tough guy to deal with, but Gary actually took care of me more than anybody else. He taught me to eat Texan-style - when he wanted dessert, he would eat the whole cake. I had never seen anything like that. For some unknown reason Gary took me under his wing (literally - he was so tall I could stand upright underneath his armpit) and tried to give me a cram course in English. I remember we stayed up until two in the morning reading Dr. Seuss books. To this day I can still do *Fox in Socks* from memory.

It was no use. Passengers would ask me questions in an assortment of languages I didn't understand and I would answer them in a language they didn't understand (even though I thought I was speaking English). Then we would all nod at each other and smile. I thought 'Hey, I'm doing pretty good so far,' but we were all just being polite. The system would have been perfect had I been working for the Russian government, but it didn't make it on Royal Caribbean. People would ask me for directions to their shore excursions and never be seen again. They're probably still wandering around some Caribbean island looking for their bus.

I also wasn't very good at following the rules laid down for the staff. In Russia, as an entertainer I could pretty much do what I wanted when I wasn't performing, but on the Royal Caribbean line, staff weren't allowed in the bars after 11:00 P.M. I was so high on the freedom I was experiencing and on the chance to be with Americans (and to meet American girls) that I kept on partying with the passengers until the wee hours. It was also the only time when my difficulties with the language weren't a problem - you'd be amazed at how bad everybody's English gets at 3:00 A.M.

It didn't take me long to figure out that my career on the high seas was going to be cut short. I knew something was up when the rest of the staff were asked their shirt sizes for the new uniforms they would be receiving for the next cruise - and nobody was asking me. I was crushed. The last day of the cruise I moped around the ship like Rush Limbaugh without Bill Clinton to kick around anymore. The next morning I packed my stuff and headed for the failure gangplank, my heart heavy. I had quit my job in Miami, my parents were still in New York and I didn't have the money to fly back. This wasn't the way I had envisioned my first cruise ship job ending.

As I was leaving, totally sad and discouraged, who should step into my path but Gary. In his hands he had an envelope, which he gave me and said, "This is from us. Keep your chin up." Inside the envelope was a letter that I still have. It was from Gary, wishing me good luck and saying he was sure he'd see me again. There was also a bunch of cash. Knowing that I had no money, Gary had collected donations from all the crew to help me get back to New York. I was touched, both by the generosity of the crew and by Gary's friendship. I did keep in touch with that lanky Texan, in fact, he was the best man at my wedding and I won't hold it against him.

Someone once wrote, "If you have one great friend, your life isn't wasted. If you have two great friends, you're a saint. If you say you have three, you're a liar."

A Shot of Smirnoff

$500 sounded fantastic. It would go a long way toward the Rolls-Royce I had my heart set on or that other luxury item I dreamt about - food. The only other way I could think of making that much money in a casino required a ski mask and Uzi.

Chapter 8

I Saw the Writing on the Wall, and It Was An Exit Sign

In the late 1970's, while the rest of the world was struggling to recover from *Saturday Night Fever,* I was working hard to become a comedian in the United States. I went to Hollywood, where aspiring, starving comedians go to become perspiring, starving comedians bussing tables. I performed my stand-up act at The Comedy Store with the likes of David Letterman, Billy

Crystal and Robin Williams. There was no doubt in my mind that the only difference between them and me was that they had managers and I didn't.

A manager is a guy who convinces you that the best way to become successful is to give him 20 percent of everything you make. I had been working as a carpenter to pay the bills (considering I worked as a carpenter by day after staying up all night performing comedy, it's a miracle I still have all my fingers). I desperately wanted to make my living as a professional comedian and I just knew that if I had a manager I could become successful.

As the "new guy in town" I was only given the late night/early morning time slots to perform my act. One night after I had done a late night show to several drunks and a guy who was taking a nap in the front row, I heard a low, rumbling voice call my name from the dark recesses of the room.

"You're a funny kid. I haven't heard anything that funny since Bill Cosby," said the raspy voice. "You should be headlining in Las Vegas." Since comedians are always looking for acceptance and admiration, this kind of compliment can go a long way.

I walked through the dimly lit room toward my new admirer. It was always dark in the club and I couldn't get a good look at his face, but we started a conversation. I felt like Mike Wallace interviewing a Mafia informant on *60 Minutes*. The shadow told me his name was Harry, that he was managing talent and wanted to take me on. He said he could get me $500 a week performing at the casinos in Las Vegas. Since I was only making $25 a show at The Comedy Store (which added up to $50 a week), $500 sounded fantastic. It would go a long way toward the Rolls Royce I had my heart set on or that other luxury item I dreamt about - food. The only other way I could think of making that much money in a casino required a ski mask and an Uzi.

The thought of performing professionally was exciting, but more important was the fact that I was going to have a manager, just like Robin Williams. Harry, the manager, told me to give him a call in one week.

I was on top of the world. I remember how thrilled I felt (just like the time I won the lottery in Russia and got three rolls of toilet paper). For the next seven days I imagined spending that $500 dozens of times. I sat back, closed my eyes and watched myself driving my Rolls Royce down Rodeo Drive. I would dine in the nicest restaurants and drink the finest wines. My career may have been shaky at that point, but my imagination was off to a great start!

I called Harry the next week. He told me to meet him in Las Vegas where he was going to introduce me to the casino owners and launch my career. I asked him how I should get to Vegas and he told me to take a bus. I didn't have a huge English vocabulary at that point, but I was pretty sure I knew what "bus" meant - and it wasn't good. This should have tipped me off to what was coming, but I was too excited about the prospect of making it big.

I spent the longest two weeks of my life on that five-hour bus trip to Vegas. I never thought humidity would be a factor inside a vehicle, but I had never been a passenger on a bus traveling in the middle of the Mojave Desert. There were 60 sweaty bodies, all measuring 98.6 degrees, on that bus and the air outside was a crisp, clear 114 degrees. I snuggled up to the passenger seated next to me just to cool off. He didn't seem to appreciate it. Harry had told me he would pick me up at the bus depot, so I knew I'd get out of the desert heat once I arrived. Surely he would have an air-conditioned limo waiting.

When I finally stepped off the bus into the blinding sunlight of the city, I searched the crowd trying to find him. Since I had only spoken to him in a dark nightclub, I really didn't know what he looked like. I was searching for somebody who looked like a successful manager and I figured Gucci shoes and a Rolex wouldn't be too hard to pick out at the Las Vegas bus depot.

As I scanned the crowd, an offensive, grimy-looking man approached me. For a moment I thought that maybe Charles Manson had been paroled. Before I could tell the panhandler that I had less money than he did, he stuck out his scaly hand and said, "Hi Yakov, I'm Harry. Glad you made it."

I stared at him in disbelief. He was the furthest thing from a Hollywood manager that I could imagine. He looked more like a used Yugo salesman who had been on a two-week bender. His hair was dyed four different shades of brown, which fortunately matched the color of his teeth - the ones that were left in his head anyway. He actually had a footprint on the back of his sports coat and his breath could have killed a water buffalo.

I knew then that I was making a mistake, but the allure of fame and fortune overshadowed the glaring warning signs that this man was not who he said he was. As we walked over to his car it became obvious that it wasn't the limo that I had imagined. I looked at the rusty heap and didn't know whether to laugh, cry or simply stop breathing. The wheels of his car (and I use the term "car" lightly here) had no hub-caps and one of the tires was actually the small donut spare they give you in case of a flat. There was mold on the floor because the convertible top didn't go up and every time it rained the car was flooded. The door wouldn't open, so in order to get into the car, I had to jump in over the top of it. We drove unevenly down the street, the car tilting to one side.

"How was your trip?" he choked out between drags on the soggy stub of a cigar.

"Keeps getting better," I said with a tone of sarcasm that was lost somewhere in the cloud of smoke.

I found myself sitting next to "Death's Stunt Double" and surrounded by nothing but scrub brush and sand. He managed to maneuver this vehicle to an off-the-strip motel where he said he booked a room. Not only was this place off the strip, it seemed like it was completely off the planet. It sure wasn't the Las Vegas Hilton. Instead of a Quality Inn, it was a Quality Out. I thought that when you put the "Do Not Disturb" sign on the front door, the cockroaches would take it down. I knew I had to get myself out of this mess, but I had no money for a hotel of my own. Even though it was obvious that this man could do little for my career, or me, I still had a faint glimmer of hope that he would somehow get me a gig in a casino.

Harry sent me into the office to get an extra key for the room. The clerk asked me how many hours I would be staying. I thought it was kind of a strange question and then I realized that some of the ladies of the evening (or women of the sidewalk or whatever you call them) were using the motel as their "office."

There were two single beds in the room and Harry told me I could sleep in one of them. I wanted to take a shower, but the water only came in a lovely selection of earth tones. At least the ice machine was convenient - it was in our closet. At that point I knew that I'd feel safer and more comfortable on the street.

We went over to a Waffle House to grab a bite to eat

that I ended up paying for with my few remaining dollars. During our meal, Harry broached the subject of legal documents. He told me that he would feel more comfortable as my manager if we had a contract. I felt like telling him that I'd feel more comfortable if he had a shower, but I couldn't stop staring at the remnants of egg that were all over his face. He reached into his pocket and produced (I know this sounds like I am making it up, but I'm not) two contracts written in pencil on Waffle House place mats. The scrawl said something about him getting 20 percent of everything I earned for the next three years. He told me to sign next to the picture of the pecan waffle, just below the smear of ketchup.

I told Harry that I appreciated what he was trying to do, but I couldn't sign the place mat without having an attorney eat off it first. I also told him that I wanted to see what he was going to actually do for me before entering into any agreement with him.

Harry was a little miffed that I wouldn't sign, but took me around to the casinos like he had promised. We pulled up to the Riviera and the valet refused to park the car. I suppose he didn't want to get his uniform dirty. I sat there while Harry went in to try and find somebody who would be interested in booking me.

We tried four or five casinos that day with no luck. He finally booked me a guest set through Sandy Hackett, Buddy Hackett's son, at the Sahara, but by the time I got on stage there were probably more people in the Sahara Desert on a hot sunny day than were sitting in the Sahara lounge. After the show, Sandy took me aside and said, "Yakov, your show was great, but what are you doing with this guy?" I told him my story. When Sandy stopped laughing, he told me this character might be able to get me a job giving blood at the Red Cross each month, but that was about it.

I confessed I had used all my money on the trip out and was staying in a room with Harry. Sandy shook his head in amazement. He then took pity on me and gave me a hotel room for the night. It was a lot better than Motel 6-Feet-Under and the water only came in one shade - clear. This unexpected gesture of kindness touched me very deeply. Sandy didn't know me from Adam, he'd only seen me do one set, yet he believed enough in me and my talent to take better care of me than I had of myself.

That night I told Harry that even though I appreciated

what he had done for me (basically exposure to head lice), but I had to move on. It was probably one of the shortest professional relationships in show biz history, next to Liz Taylor's marriages.

The next morning I packed my bag and headed to the bus station. On the trip back to Los Angeles, I thought about the reason I had gotten myself into that mess. It was because I had let my overwhelming desire get in the way of making a clear decision. I thought getting a manager would mean I was a real comedian in real show business, when in fact being a real comedian meant writing material and working on my craft.

The part of my brain that tells me when a situation isn't right took a nap during that trip to Vegas, but those couple of days in the desert turned out to be an opportunity after all. Since then, I always watch for the warning signs of something that is too good to be true, like the motel sign which reads, "Presidential Suite $19.95." Now when I see an opportunity, I think it through before I make a decision. I'm in no hurry to jump feet first into quicksand, whether it's in Las Vegas, Los Angeles or anywhere else.

A Shot of Smirnoff

Here I was finally a free man, in prison.

Chapter 9

Europe On Five Jails a Day

Sometimes the most exciting adventures of our lives take place when we least expect. Most of the time though, when we are faced with a situation that isn't planned, we panic. I've learned that in order to grow as individuals we must embrace the unexpected as comfortably as we do the predictable. I first realized this while attempting a trip to Germany in 1979.

After being in America for a couple of years, I wanted something that every patriotic American wants - a foreign car. You have to remember, this was the late 1970s. During that time America was known more for pet rocks than manufacturing the finest automobiles (remember the Ford Pinto?). I had my heart set on a Mercedes-Benz 450SL, but since I was just starting my comedy career, the only German vehicle in my price range was a ten year-old Volkswagen Beetle and that was only if I leased it. Since the Beetle really wasn't a "chick magnet" (as important to me as an engine in those days), I opted for the Mercedes. As you can probably tell, my priorities then were more materialistic than they are now.

A Russian friend of mine, David, told me that we each could purchase a used Mercedes in Germany for about half of what it would cost in the U.S. Shipping the vehicles back wouldn't be that expensive and we could be driving the cars of our dreams in a couple of weeks. I had learned in Russia it's always better to visit Germans than have Germans visit you. I was really excited about getting a car and it was the first time I was going to travel abroad as an American - or so I thought. The plan was for

David and me to kick a few tires, make our respective deals and be home in a week. No problem. I bought a ticket from New York to London to Frankfurt, Germany. It was a discount ticket - between London and Frankfurt, I had to change planes in Atlanta. I brought with me everything I needed to visit Germany: a German phrase book, some Deutschmarks and a pair of one size fits all lederhosen.

David and I flew into Heathrow International Airport outside of London. We thought all we had to do was clear customs and then fly on to Frankfurt. The customs official in London greeted me with a crooked English smile and asked to see my passport, but I had no passport of any kind. When we left Russia, the government took our passports away from us and since I hadn't officially become a naturalized U.S. citizen, I only had a resident alien document, which I gladly handed over to the customs officer. His toothy grin vanished as quickly as a pint of beer in a pub on a Friday evening. He told me that I had to have a passport or a visa to get into Germany. Otherwise, I'd have to fly back to the United States.

I couldn't believe the irony. My whole life I wanted desperately to get into the United States and now I couldn't get out! I contacted German officials who told me it would take two weeks to get a visa to enter the country. I figured my own country would help so I called the American Embassy. The first thing they asked me was "Are you an American citizen?"

I told them, "Not yet, but I'm working on it."

"Well, call us when you're done. For now, you're on your own." I guess when it comes to visas there's a difference between a full-fledged American and one still under construction.

Since David had no documentation either, both of us had to return to the United States. The last flight for New York had already departed and the customs official said, with a charming British lilt, "I'm afraid you'll have to spend the night in detention." I was hoping this was some continental-sounding hotel name, like "De Hilton," but it turned out to be what I feared, de jail. I was told we would be deported back to America the next day by teatime.

By this point I was desperate. I pleaded with him, "But I'm going to buy a Mercedes-Benz in Germany." That seemed to inspire some compassion because he managed to spit out, "pity," as two burly security officers led us away. Soon we were sitting in an immigration prison with several other men who obviously weren't going to be buying a Mercedes that day either.

David was really depressed about the whole situation and mumbled, "It was worth a shot." Trying to brighten his mood, I said, "Look on the bright side. We're in England, we just got to meet the queen and he seems pretty friendly." Then I added, "There must be a country that will let us in without a visa. We'll just find another way into Germany."

I laid down on the metal cot and started thinking about what was going on. Here I was, finally a free man, in prison. I started laughing out loud. David got the giggles and the two of us began chortling like a couple of school kids. The other inmates thought we were psychotic and I'm sure they were afraid to fall asleep before we did.

The next morning we were escorted to the airplane and British officials made sure that we boarded. On the flight back, David was still upset that we had wasted our money on a flight for nothing, but I told him I wasn't quitting until I got myself a Mercedes.

Back in New York, I called the embassies of countries

that were closest to Germany and asked how long it would take to get a visa. The Belgian Embassy told us we would get one that same day. Finally! Someone was speaking my language (well, actually it was French, but it sounded pretty good so I went along with it). In any event, I had my new plan. We could fly to Brussels and take the train to Germany. I thought we could just walk right into Germany, considering how Germany had marched right into Belgium.

David and I flew to Brussels and entered the country with our Belgian visas. We had a quick Belgian waffle and then boarded a train to Germany. Later, a friend asked me why we didn't just buy a Mercedes in Belgium. I quickly responded, "Good question. With friends like you, who needs a mother-in-law?"

The train arrived at the Belgian-German border. Just when we thought we were home free, two German soldiers boarded the train. They were dressed in full uniform and carried menacing-looking machine guns (as opposed to the more friendly-looking variety of automatic weapon). They were demanding passports from everyone. David and I were getting really nervous as the soldiers approached. They loomed over us like two oak trees on a windy day.

"Passports!" they snapped.

I told the angry-looking soldier that we were just passing through, like Germany told Poland in 1939 (of course the latter part of that remark stayed in my head where it belonged).

"Where are you going?" the German soldier barked.

I don't know why I said this, but I sputtered, "We're going to Holland."

"You are on the wrong train." Then the soldiers stepped out of our compartment and signaled for us to get off. As a Russian, I know that there is no greater feeling of sheer terror than a German soldier directing you to get on or off a train. The soldiers took us to the Immigration Office where once again we had to stay in jail. There was a train leaving for Amsterdam in a couple of hours and we were going to be on it. I started looking around in vain for the Ford Pinto dealership.

The next morning we arrived in Amsterdam. I didn't want to go through German customs again without the proper documentation, so we went to the German Embassy in Holland. We approached a man at the counter who told us we could get German visitor visas in two days. He leaned towards us and said that for a $200 “processing fee” we could get them in an hour. We both paid the man cash and the only “processing” he did was to slip the money into his pocket. I’m sure he filled out the proper paperwork right after lunch.

We took yet another train and finally got into Germany legally (sort of). Once there, we picked up a couple of newspapers and started looking for a car. Since neither of us spoke German, the negotiations for our vehicles were conducted mostly in sign language. I settled on a lime-yellow Mercedes-Benz 450SL. It was fully loaded, including heated seats (something sure to come in handy during those frequent midsummer L.A. snow squalls). We made the arrangements to have our cars shipped back to the U.S. and we flew back to New York. When we arrived at U.S. Immigration, the officer said, “Welcome home.” I was so excited I almost kissed him, but opted instead to kiss the ground.

I look back on that trip with fond memories. A lot of people like to tour Europe by rail, but in my case it turned out to be “Europe by jail.” However, I learned how important the element of adventure is in one's life. Facing the unknown is an excellent way to realize your potential and experience the thrill and empowerment of overcoming a challenging situation. Sometimes as adults we mistakenly trade excitement and unpredictability for security and comfort, but it is through adventure that we can have new experiences that allow us to grow as individuals and perhaps become more open-minded, allowing us to entertain new thoughts and ideas.

Of course, it would be nice to have both comfort and adventure. I suppose if somebody could attach a five-speed transmission, sport suspension and a 250 horsepower engine to a La-Z-Boy recliner and have it parked in Britney Spears' garage, most men would be happy forever.

A Shot of Smirnoff

Getting lessons about dating from Andrew Dice Clay is like getting anger management advice from Mike Tyson.

Chapter 10

A Master's Degree in Laughter from a "Fraternity" of Comedians

When I moved to Hollywood with my dreams of becoming a successful comedian I began meeting many other hopefuls. Most of us eventually achieved some degree of commercial success.

I'm proud to say that wonderful friendships developed between many of us, an informal fraternity of comedians. We came to know that success was really something you achieved by being true to yourself.

I did some of my first comedy showcases at The Comedy Store in Los Angeles. A wonderful woman named Mitzy Shore ran this. After my first showcase, she invited me back to perform regularly. I was sharing the stage with people like Jay Leno, Billy Crystal, David Letterman, Richard Pryor and Robin Williams.

There was a house on the hill above The Comedy Store and Mitzy Shore made it affordable to many of the beginning comedians that were performing at her club. Most of the time there were up to five of us sharing the space (it still was better than the 25 people to an apartment I was used to in Russia). The Comedy Store house was like the world's most out-of-control fraternity. I think they must have used it for the model for John Belushi's movie, *Animal House*. It's the only place where you could learn how to jump a motorcycle from the dining room to the kitchen. The parties in that house would go on to the wee hours of the morning. I would get up in the morning and have to pick up empty beer cans and greasy pizza boxes. I always wiped off the dusty mirror and hung it back up on the wall. I was so naive, I thought they were using the mirror as a tray for powdered donuts.

I met one of my roommates the first day I moved in. When I walked in it was kind of dark and I saw a lump of black leather with a cigarette sticking out. I thought the couch was on fire and then I realized it was Andrew Dice Clay. Andrew later became very well known as the "dirty nursery rhyme" guy, but at the time he was still as "undiscovered" as I was. He got up from the sofa and introduced himself, saying, "I'm Andrew Dice Clay." I thought he was kidding so I said, "My name is Yakov Craps Smirnoff." He wasn't laughing and I thought I'd get the craps beaten out of me.

We actually hit it off pretty good because we were both foreigners: I was from Russia and he was from Brooklyn. We became friends and he volunteered to show me around Los Angeles. However, he was homesick for New York, so we'd drive around in his green convertible with the white interior and he would throw out candy wrappers, soda cans, half-eaten cheeseburgers and so forth. Once I said,

"Andrew, what are you doing? You're littering!" He replied, "Hey, I want this place to look like Brooklyn. This is not littering - this is decorating."

I did make one big mistake, I asked Andrew to give me advice about meeting women. Getting lessons about dating from Andrew Dice Clay is like getting anger management tips from Mike Tyson. I asked him, "Where do you meet women?" He said, "I meet women when I do my laundry." I did his laundry for a month and I still wasn't meeting anybody. I told him, "I'm not meeting anyone," and he said, "Well, you've got to go where women are. Do you like wildlife?" I said, "Yes," so he took me to Hooters Restaurant. I didn't see any owls, all I saw was men with big eyes who could spin their heads all the way around.

I did manage to start dating and I had a few relationships that were serious. I remember asking Andrew how I should break up with a girl I'd been dating. He took me out to get her what he called a "going-away" present - only he had me pick out a ring. I showed it to another roommate, Tom Wilson (who played Biff in all the *Back to the Future* movies). Tom stopped me before I made an irreversible mistake, saying, "Yakov, this is an engagement ring." I said, "But Andrew told me to buy it." Tom laughed and joked, "Andrew is not a representative of the human race."

I did manage to get Andrew back for the practical jokes he loved to play on me. Few people knew that behind that tough-guy exterior, the real Andrew was a pussycat with a big heart. Andrew also believed in ghosts. We tied a fishing line to a rocking chair that sat across from the sofa in the living room. As Andrew sat on the sofa, watching TV, we'd pull on the fishing line and the rocking chair would rock - without anyone seemingly in it. For two years Andrew was convinced our house was haunted and he paid homage to what he thought were the ghosts of past comedians.

I learned many valuable things from Andrew. If you have frozen waffles, but no syrup, Dr. Pepper is a reasonable substitute. Bus exhaust has vitamins in it. It's fine, at Thanksgiving, to have a slice of pizza while eating turkey. Finally, when an actress enters a scene in a movie, yelling, "Nice jugs!" shows your friends that you appreciate fine art.

Andrew's big break came when he was featured on Rodney Dangerfield's *Young Comedians* HBO special. His raunchy nursery rhymes brought down the house and for a while he was the leader of a whole group of "shock" comedians. I remember the first time I saw his show after he'd "made it." He performed in the L.A. Coliseum and eighteen thousand people were screaming his name. I couldn't help feeling that even though he had made his mark, the Andrew I saw on stage that night wasn't the Andrew I knew.

Watching Andrew confirmed for me that I had to stick to my own truth, the kind of comedy that worked for my personality and the audiences I wanted to attract. My decision to follow my own road has served me well. I also witnessed how well it served another young comedian who was a Comedy Store graduate.

In the early 1980s my career was doing well. I had gone from showcases at The Comedy Store to a household name almost overnight. When I was touring the U.S. as a headliner, appearing in Las Vegas, Chicago, New York, L.A., Miami (all big cities), occasionally I had a young comedian as my opening act. We would be driving around town at one tour stop or another and this guy would stop the car every other mile so he could write down a funny thought.

I never saw anyone work so hard polishing his act as this young man. He was very clear on where he was headed. He'd already been offered several television series, but had turned them down because of creative differences.

When I heard this, I was shocked. It took real courage and vision to turn down a TV series, with its steady money and national exposure. I, on the other hand, took the first show that was offered to me. Certainly, I was motivated by the money, but I also think I was just afraid to say no. So I did a show called *What a Country* in 1985. It was a first run syndicated series that lasted twenty-six episodes. It went off the air after one season.

Meanwhile, this hardworking young man kept doing his act on the road and saying no to several sitcom proposals. He decided to go to the networks with his own idea for his television series. Four years later, America was introduced to Jerry Seinfeld.

I couldn't have been happier for Jerry, because I knew how hard he had worked to get to that point. Even more, I was glad because he did it on his own terms. Jerry stuck to his own ideas of what was funny, believing that there was an audience for his kind of humor. Boy, was there ever! *Seinfeld* lasted for nine seasons and is like the Energizer

Bunny; it keeps going and going in syndication. Based on the reruns, I don't think I can afford for Jerry Seinfeld to open for me any time soon.

It felt good to celebrate Jerry's success. The standard picture of show business and comedians is everybody for himself. Sure, we are competitive, but ultimately it's about competing with yourself, to become the best you can be. I believe that when we compete with ourselves to do our best, nobody loses and we all win.

I saw this spirit of competition clearly in another context years later watching Oprah Winfrey. She had a program on the Special Olympics. These are games where physically handicapped children from all over the U.S. come together and compete in different sports. Oprah showed a bunch of kids lined up for the 100-yard dash. Their faces were so determined, so excited, really into it. Each of them had the "eye of the tiger." They could have put Rocky to shame. He would have looked like a pussycat.

The starting gun went off and the children shot out of the blocks like they were running against Carl Lewis. The runners were bunched together, heading for the finish line, turning the corner neck and neck, when one of them fell. All the other kids stopped, walked back and helped the fallen child back to his feet. They continued the race and all crossed the finish line together.

When I told this story to my daughter, Natasha, she said to me, "Daddy, I know why they call it the Special Olympics."

"Why?" I asked.

"Because the athletes care more about each other than they do about winning!"

Bill Cosby, a great comedian, has an interesting philosophy: he doesn't like to accept awards. Bill told me he doesn't believe in that kind of competition. "Don't worry about winning," he said. "Just do the best you can do and you'll always be a winner."

My comedian friends have taught me a lot and not just how to pick up girls or how to jump motorcycles indoors (in Andrew's case, how to eat spaghetti and meatballs without spitting out your gum). Comedians helped me learn the real meaning of competition, the Special Olympics kind. You do your best and you cheer on the next guy who's doing his best, too. As Andrew used to remind me, "Yakov, it ain't who you are. It's what you do with what you've got."

A Shot of Smirnoff

It's amazing how one, thirty-second beer commercial could open more doors than years of hard work. I guess that's why college kids spend so much time at fraternity parties.

Chapter 11

Turning Stumbling Blocks into Stepping Stones, or How I Broke Red Skelton's Hip

Being turned down by *The Tonight Show* turned out to be a blessing in disguise. That may sound sarcastic, but it's true. You don't get discovered and then become great; you become great and then you get discovered. Not being on *The Tonight Show* taught me that sometimes what appears to be stumbling blocks might actually be stepping-stones.

In the early 1980s, I was performing at comedy clubs all across the country and was a regular at the Comedy Store in Los Angeles. The Comedy Store was the Microsoft of the comedy business and tougher to break into than Bill Gates' e-mail account. Though I was happy to be performing there, I still had not achieved the one benchmark by which all comedians measure their success- an appearance on *The Tonight Show*.

I had auditioned several times for Jim McCauley, the show's talent coordinator, who was in charge of selecting comedians to perform on the program. Jim didn't like my act. I would do my six-minute routine for Jim at The Comedy Store and he would reject me. I'd change my act and show it to him again. Again he would reject me. After numerous calls and correspondences, Jim McCauley finally gave me some hope. He told me, "You'll be on *The Tonight Show* when hell freezes over." Every night for weeks, I checked the Weather Channel and found out that hell doesn't get much coverage. The rumor was that no cooling trends were forecast for the Greater Hell Metropolitan Area.

It was depressing knowing that unless the Devil began wearing long-johns, I would not be appearing on *The Tonight Show*. As long as Jim McCauley was the gatekeeper, I had to try and find a way to climb the fence. I did everything I could to convince him I was right for the show. I kept in touch and sent him gifts and flowers on special occasions. The years went by and I occasionally thought about *The Tonight Show*. By "occasionally," I mean every weeknight at 11:30 P.M. and 10:30 P.M. when I traveled the Midwest.

I resolved not getting on *The Tonight Show* in my mind by convincing myself that Jim McCauley would never like me and *The Tonight Show* was a small part of show business. I decided that whatever is meant to be is meant to be and I moved on.

My career began to flourish. I headlined the big rooms in Las Vegas. I had parts in three movies: *Heartburn* with Meryl Streep and Jack Nicholson, *Moscow on the Hudson* with Robin Williams and *The Money Pit* with Tom Hanks. After working with me, all four of those actors went on to win Oscars and still no calls from *The Tonight Show*.

Working in the movies took my mind off *The Tonight Show* for a while. I didn't let it bother me until I realized that out of five of us, only Streep, Hanks, Nicholson and Williams could get on *The Tonight Show* whenever they liked.

Miller Brewing Company then hired me to appear in a Miller Lite commercial. As far as life-changing events are concerned, a beer commercial may not rank up there with the Nobel Prize or a burning bush, but it worked for me.

The commercial was set in a bar, surrounded by a group of happy people. I poured a glass of beer and said, "In America, you can always find a party. In Russia, the party always finds you." The commercial was a smashing success for Miller and for me. Guess what? Johnny Carson, the host of *The Tonight Show*, saw my commercial and thought I was funny. For a comedian, that's like finding out that Jennifer Garner, Cameron Diaz and Penelope Cruz think you're cute.

One 30-second beer commercial could open more doors than years of hard work. Maybe that's why college kids spend so much time at fraternity parties. The next day I received word from Comedy Store owner Mitzy Shore that Jim McCauley had been looking for me. Johnny Carson wanted me on the show right away. It had taken almost six years, but hell had finally frozen over. To be perfectly honest, my first thought was to not do the show out of spite. That thought lasted for about two seconds. I called McCauley and asked if I could appear on Thanksgiving. He said, “Nobody tells me when they’re getting on the show, but you can come in and we’ll discuss it.”

I met Jim in his office and I explained that appearing on Thanksgiving made a lot of sense to me because I had so much to be thankful for since coming to America. Jim was concerned that it wouldn’t go over with the audience, but now that Johnny wanted me I used my leverage.

Jim reluctantly agreed to schedule me to appear the night before Thanksgiving. My friend, Jimmy Brogan, (who later worked nine years for *The Tonight Show*) accompanied me to NBC Studios in Burbank, California. Brogan told me that if Johnny waved me over to the couch after my set, I shouldn’t wait for him to ask me a question but just jump in with a joke. Johnny had only called two or three first-time guests over to the couch in the history of *The Tonight Show*, I wasn't too worried about it, but over and over I pictured myself being called over to the couch.

On the night of the show my heart was pounding like a jackhammer. Johnny introduced me and I'll never forget walking out on stage and performing for that live audience and the tens of millions at home watching in bed (that must be a really big bed). Every joke got a huge laugh and applause. At the end of my monologue, I shared the story with the audience about how my parents and I had our first Thanksgiving in America.

When we came to America, people told us about Thanksgiving, the holiday where the Pilgrims and Indians got together and agreed to build a casino. They said that this is the time when everybody gives thanks for the freedom and opportunity and all the things that we have in this country, but it seemed to me that it wasn't enough just to say thanks. My parents and I celebrated our first Thanksgiving in our little apartment in New York. We had a meal and we all joined hands as my father said a prayer for good food and health. Then something happened. Instead of releasing our hands we couldn't let go. We kept holding on to each other tighter and tighter, because we realized we were together and free, really free. Here were three adults looking for a way to express our appreciation and we didn't know how. I said, now I know how to say it. It's 'thanks.'

My story struck a chord with the audience. The response was overwhelming and Johnny waved me over to the couch. When I sat down I immediately said, "Johnny, I have to tell you, I love this country. You have so many things we never had in Russia. Like the police here have warning shots." Johnny laughed so hard he almost fell out of his chair. During the commercial break, Jim McCauley ran over to me and asked if I could appear again the very next week. I thanked him, but said I'd like to pace myself and would do it in a few months.

A few years after my *Tonight Show* appearance, I had the opportunity to meet the great comedian, Red Skelton. The first thing he said to me was, "For a long time, I was thinking about suing you."

I asked, "Why?"

"I was lying in bed watching you on *The Tonight Show*," Red replied in mock anger. "When you told the joke about the police having warning shots, I laughed so hard I fell out of bed and broke my hip!" Naturally I felt bad about that, but I couldn't help but feel a little bit proud that I broke a legendary comedian's hip with one punch (line).

I appeared on *The Tonight Show* six times over the next few years and I know that those appearances helped my career immeasurably (and possibly broke every bone in Red Skelton's body). Each time, I would discuss the jokes with Jim McCauley, who would give me his opinion. Jim helped me put together the best set possible. The man I once considered an adversary was now helping me do the best job I could.

Everything in nature has a time when it's ready to emerge into the world. Pick a flower before it's ready to bloom, the flower will likely die before it has a chance to show its beauty. Life isn't supposed to be a struggle. If you want a struggle, try squeezing into a pair of jeans you wore back when you were 21. When I'm in a situation where I want something that is out of my reach, I reflect on my experiences with Jim McCauley and know that it's not yet quite my time to bloom. It was frustrating to wait, but I am glad my *Tonight Show* break came when it did and not before. If it had taken any longer, though, people might have mistaken me for George Burns.

Got It

When Life Points a Finger at You, It's Usually the Middle One

A Shot of Smirnoff

Let's face it. If it hadn't been for a long line of "dreamers", I would have written this book with a goose feather, and you would be reading it by candle-light while your husband cleans his false teeth with sandpaper.

Chapter 12

Sometimes It Takes a Nightmare to Realize a Dream

It has been said that everything that has ever been created or accomplished in the universe started out as an idea. Some of those - like the "creative accounting" at Enron - didn't work out so well. We all, at some point, have had an idea which caused a light bulb to go on in our heads. Except Thomas Edison who, I suppose, had a candle flare up when he thought of the light bulb.

Those ideas that swirl around in our brains are simply a form of energy. The recliners we sit on, the televisions we watch, the Doritos we eat and the Stairmaster we stare at, all started out as a thought, a piece of energy in someone's noggin. If that energy is applied in the right way, it can manifest as something tangible.

I have been and always will be a dreamer and I find it sad that the term is usually applied in a negative way. Let's face it, if it hadn't been for a long line of "dreamers," I would have written this book with a goose feather and you'd be reading it by candlelight while your husband cleaned his false teeth with a piece of sandpaper.

My dreams of owning a big home in America started when I was living in a communal apartment building in Odessa, a city on the Black Sea coast. My family shared living accommodations with nine other families in a place that was once, prior to the Russian revolution, home to only one wealthy family. During the communist regime, more than twenty people called one floor of this three story brick building home.

One of the worst things about living in a communal apartment was that all nine families had to share the same bathroom. Having a single water closet for nine families meant long line-ups and constant bickering. On the positive side, it also meant a consistently warm toilet seat. When I immigrated to the United States, it was natural that I wanted to pursue my dream of owning a huge home with cold toilet seats.

When I moved from New York to Los Angeles to pursue my comedy career, I knew I had to get a place of my own. My parents had made the move with me to Los Angeles and to be quite honest, they were becoming bored. My mother and father were both officially retired and they took up a hobby. That hobby was "driving me crazy." While I admired their natural abilities at this, I desperately wanted to help them diversify their interests.

My father was handy and my mother was never afraid of a little hard work. I thought I could kill two birds with one stone, so to speak. I planned to buy a fixer-upper for myself and have my parents do the "fixer-upping." This would keep them focused on something other than me while converting this house into my dream home. I knew exactly what I wanted. The house had to be big, with a view of Hollywood. It had to be on a substantial piece of property.

The yard had to have a beautiful pool that featured live pink flamingoes and peacocks roaming the landscaped yard. Just for fun, several beautiful women would feed me grapes and fan me with palm leaves (hey, it's my dream!). The price I envisioned was $120,000. Your reaction to this figure will depend on what part of the country you live in. I know that in parts of the Midwest, a $120,000 home makes you the Donald Trump of the neighborhood. In Los Angeles, $120,000 would get you an option on Steven Spielberg's doghouse.

A realtor happened to be in my neighborhood. She saw me out in the yard, walked over and asked to borrow a hammer to pound a "For Sale" sign into the yard across the street. I took a chance at being ridiculed and shared my dream with her. I went on to describe the house I wanted and told her what my price range was. I thought she was going to hit me with the hammer, but instead she said, "I think I might have something for you." Of course, this is the first line a realtor is taught to say, so I didn't expect to hear from her.

Much to my surprise, she called me the next day to schedule a viewing of a home in Hollywood Hills that at one time had belonged to Lenny Bruce. Lenny Bruce was a famous comedian in the 1960s that, after a turbulent life and career, committed suicide. When I saw the house, I had an insight into what might have prompted Lenny to do himself in. When the realtor told me we were having a "viewing," I didn't realize that she meant that it was a wake. The house was a real disaster. There was a swimming pool, but it was unintentional thanks to the plumbing (or lack of it). The basement was filled with water, complete with floating furniture. While I'd always wanted a waterbed, this wasn't what I had in mind. There were no pink flamingoes, but I did see a cockroach the size of a peacock.

When I say this was a "fixer-upper," it's a bit like saying that Chernobyl needed a little sprucing up. However, the price was right, so I told the surprised realtor that this was exactly what I'd been dreaming of. She raised an eyebrow and asked if I knew any other Russian immigrants who were in the market for a home.

I started the long, drawn out procedure of purchasing the real estate that was as foreign to me as it is to Americans. I still don't understand "closing costs" - they ought to call them "opening costs," because every ten minutes I had to open my checkbook and spend more money. I forged ahead but ran into a small stumbling block while going through escrow. It seemed that a two-foot wide swath of the property was still owned by the previous homeowner. That piece of real estate connected my front door to the sidewalk. I had two choices: buy the property back or take up pole-vaulting. Pole-vaulting would have been easier.

I had a little trouble tracking down the owner of this sliver of land because he had been relocated, with the assistance of the justice system, to the local penitentiary. He had lost the house to his attorney but retained a controlling interest in that strip. At that point most people with any sense would have walked away from a mess like that, but I felt I was getting closer to my goal all the time.

I went to visit the owner of that tiny piece of property in the Crowbar Carlton. When I met the guy in the visitor's room, I explained the situation and offered him five hundred dollars for his property. He said, "Fifty."

"Fifty thousand, are you crazy?" I blurted out, then quickly changed my tone - after all, I was talking to a criminal who might get out of this place someday.

"No. Fifty dollars," he responded quietly. "I'm only allowed to have fifty dollars on me while I'm in prison."

"I can do that," I said with a sigh of relief. I dug into my wallet and realized that the $500 I had brought with me was all in hundred dollar bills. I tried to slide him the hundred under the glass, but he shook his head. "Fifty or no deal," he reiterated.

I thought it wouldn't be a problem to get change and I started asking around. Once again, there was the naive immigrant, this time waving a hundred dollar bill in the middle of the prison asking for change. Fortunately, one of the guards could break the hundred for me. I paid the convict his fifty and he signed off on the deed. I was one short step closer to owning the home and fifty long steps to getting the heck out of that joint!

In any event, escrow closed on the house and I moved in. Moving in didn't take long - thanks to my down payment and all the closing costs, my furniture now consisted of a table, a chair and the back seat of my car, which I slept in. I lived amongst the renovations and for a while none of the four toilets were working. How ironic - I finally live in a country that has plenty of toilet paper and the toilets don't work.

In the middle of the renovations, I landed a role in *The Money Pit*, a movie starring Tom Hanks and Shelley Long. The movie was about a young couple that buys a fixer-upper. I wasn't surprised that I got the role - after all, I'd been living the part for three years. I could've written the script myself, but it would have been rated "R" because of the language the contractors were using. Plus, the amount of money I'd spent on my house was more than the film's entire budget. The couple in the film ends up separating because of the stress of the renovations. After what I went through, I believe that renovating a home can indeed be the cause of divorce. I had no such luck - after the renovations my parents were still with me.

I would go to the set in the morning to work on the movie and come home to my little hole in the ground to work on my dream at night. During the renovations of my home, I slipped and fell right on my Ukraine (that's Russian for "where the sun don't shine"). That week, we shot a scene in the movie where Tom Hanks falls through the rotten floor of the fixer-upper. Everybody thought it was hilarious except me because I still had the bruise on my buttocks reminding me that while "art" might be funny, life sometimes wasn't.

With the help of my parents, I - against all odds - finished the project. I had achieved my dream, a huge house with a pool and exotic birds. The girls with the grapes never showed up, but two out of three ain't bad. I had tangible proof that dreams do come true. It all began with an idea, an invisible piece of energy in my head that eventually was transformed into my home.

Of course, not all my dreams are of material things. I have created my own career in America and have a very happy life. I've visualized these things and with hard work, good friends and my family, I've been fortunate enough to achieve them.

No matter what you want in your life, if you see it, live it, smell it, feel it and taste it, you can attain it. Remember, all of mankind's achievements started as nothing more than an idea in the mind of a dreamer. If I could just envision myself six inches taller ...

A Shot of Smirnoff

I was a little older than Brooke so to make myself look younger, I made a point of standing as close as I could to Bob Hope.

Chapter 13

Dating Brooke Shields is a Tall Order

I dated several women in America, but no one really clicked for me. Then one day I saw Brook Shields on the cover of *Bride Magazine* in a beautiful white wedding dress and said to myself, "I want to marry her. She's already got the dress." Now I was probably not the only guy in the world who wanted to marry Brooke Shields, but I am probably the only guy who was foolish enough to announce it on national television. Of course, I never really thought I would meet her.

Several months later, my agent called and asked if I'd like to be on the Bob Hope television special. When I got to the rehearsal I could hardly believe my eyes. Sitting right across the room was the woman of my dreams, Brooke Shields. It turned out that Brooke was a regular on Bob Hope's comedy specials. When Brooke saw me she jumped up from the table and headed straight for me. Imagine a 6 foot tall model charging at me. I thought I was going to be the runway. At first I thought she was going to slug me because of my brash comments on the talk show, but it was quite the opposite. She was smiling as she introduced herself. I knew that I was a little older than Brooke, so to make myself look younger, I made a point of standing as close as I could to Bob Hope.

Later, Brooke invited me to her dressing room where she told me that she knew about my crush on her. It was really quite embarrassing and I was ready to apologize when she told me she thought I was cute. She liked the fact that I was not afraid to express my feelings and I was willing to say what I wanted and go after it. Then she gave me three phone numbers and said, "Call me tomorrow." When Brooke Shields gives you three phone numbers it's time to buy lottery tickets. When a woman gives me her phone number, it is normally for Taco Bell.

I wanted to play it cool, so I didn't call her until 7:05 the next morning. We set up a lunch date. Good thing there's no such thing as the "Brain Police" - if anyone knew what was going on in my head I would have been arrested for indecent exposure.

My date with Brooke was like something out of a classic romance film. I picked her up in my convertible and we drove with the top down along the Pacific Coast Highway. The view to my right was breathtaking and the ocean was okay, too. It was hard for me to keep my eyes on the road, but we made it to a vegetarian restaurant in Brentwood that Brooke had recommended. She ordered several dishes that were new to me, but I was game to try anything. She was a vegetarian and ordered hummus. When it arrived, she asked me what I thought of it. I told her, "It looks like a combination of mayonnaise and dirt." Luckily, she laughed. Trying to be polite, I ate some of the hummus. Brooke asked what I thought of the taste. I said it tasted like a combination of mayonnaise and dirt. It was great to watch her laugh. Brooke also ordered soy milk. I asked her "How do you milk soy?" She said, "you get a little chair and you pull on the tiny soy utters," and proceeded to show me how to milk soy. We both had a great time and laughed a lot. I drove Brooke back home and as we were saying goodbye, she kissed me on the cheek. I'm glad I was standing on the curb; otherwise she would have kissed me on the top of my head.

Brooke told me she'd like to see me again and she'd also like me to meet her mother. I was on top of the world (well, I was on top of the curb anyway). The woman of my dreams had just kissed me and I vowed never to shave my cheek again (as you can see I haven't). I got in my car and drove off. The sun was setting as I drove down the coast. I kept looking at myself in the rear view mirror and repeating, "Bond, James Bond."

I didn't know it at the time, but my time as 007 would be short-lived. For our second date Brooke and I met at the exclusive, five-star restaurant that her mother had selected. It was a very fancy place. Everyone was wearing suits and eating unrecognizable food. This time I was more anxious than excited. Now that my fantasy was a reality I felt I was in over my head and drowning quickly. Even *Baywatch* couldn't save me.

I was so desperate to make a good impression on Brooke's mom and was so nervous that everything went wrong. I told the waiter that I'll have what Mrs. Shields was having. For an appetizer the waiter brought a metal plate that looked like a hubcap from a small French car with oily things in it. As I put one of them in my mouth I asked the waiter what I was eating. He said, "Escargot." I said, "What is Escargot?" He said, "They are snails." That snail flew out of my mouth. I have never seen a snail move so fast. I tried to make conversation, but I sensed immediately that Mrs. Shields didn't approve of me. I suppose I wasn't the man she envisioned her daughter being with. She asked a lot of questions about how I got out of Russia. Did I have the legal papers and what was my status? For a moment I thought she was building a case to have me deported. The rest of the lunch felt like an IRS audit. No one was laughing. When we were saying good-bye there was no kiss on the cheek from Brooke, just a superficial Hollywood hug! I got in my car and looked at myself in the rearview mirror, and said "Dork, Big Dork." I did learn something. That is why God created Adam and Eve, not Adam, Eve and her mother.

A Shot of Smirnoff

On the golf course, James Garner was tall, debonair and handsome. I was convinced we were from the same gene pool. "Maybe you should read the green," he said. "I think I'll wait for the movie to come out," I innocently replied.

Chapter 14

True Charity (and Fruitcake) Will Always Come Back

It's been said that there are two kinds of charity in this world. The first one is charity with an expected return, such as donating to a telethon just to see your name flash across the television screen. The second is giving anonymously with no expectation of getting a return.

In my life I have participated in both types. Making a contribution under the disguise of "charity" and expecting something in return feels like a somewhat shady business deal. Instead, it's the anonymous variety of charity that has brought me the most happiness. The spirit of giving is just as important as the donation itself.

When I was still living in Hollywood, I was trying to sell a movie script called *First Son*. It was a comedy about the illegitimate son of the president of the United States who wreaks havoc in the White House (during some presidential administrations, it might have been a documentary). I wanted to star in the movie and I knew that if I could get a well-known actor to play the president, it would be far easier to get the movie made. I thought that James Garner would make a perfect president and father to my character. He was tall, debonair and handsome. I was convinced we were from the same gene pool. The only problem was, I didn't know James Garner.

I suppose I could have just called James Garner's agent, but that would have been far too easy. Instead, I attended a celebrity auction. One of the items on the program was a brand new set of golf clubs and a round of eighteen holes with James Garner at the Bel-Air Country Club. The purpose of this charity event was to raise money to save the whales, but I was trying to catch a big fish of my own.

The auctioneer announced, "A golf game with Mr. James Garner, star of 'The Rockford Files.' We will start the bidding at one thousand dollars."

I bid first thinking there'd be little or no competition, but before long, I was in a heated battle with one of the former stars of *Charlie's Angels*, Cheryl Ladd. Apparently she had a script to sell, too.

It wasn't long before the bidding reached four thousand dollars. I glanced over at Cheryl and she leered back at me as if to say, "Don't make me get Charlie on the phone!" She threw her hand up in the air and shouted, "Forty-two hundred."

I quickly countered, "Five thousand!" There was hush over the crowd and for a moment I, along with everyone else in the room, wondered what moron had bid five grand just to play one round of golf.

"Going once, twice, three times. Five thousand to the winner, Yakov Smirnoff."

I was stunned. I also thought that for five grand they should throw in Cheryl Ladd. As I wrote out the check it occurred to me that I probably could have joined Bel-Air Country Club for the same amount. Nevertheless, my plan was coming together and there was only one minor problem to overcome - I had never golfed before. How tough could it be? It seemed to me that the biggest challenge to playing golf was understanding the language. In any other situation, if a man asked me what kind of shaft did I have and how many strokes did I need, I'd punch him out.

Even though I was a "golf virgin," I didn't think golfing would be that difficult. I'd just buy some checkered pants, a pair of goofy shoes and learn some new multi-syllable curse words. I was just excited about the possibility of spending four hours selling James Garner on my script. Getting him alone on the golf course would be the perfect place to convince him to star in my movie.

It was time to put the rest of my plan into action. My first move was to postpone the game because I really needed to learn how to golf. I took daily lessons for two months, which cost another several hundred dollars. My game didn't improve, but I did manage to drive two golf pros to teach tennis instead. After countless reminders of "keep your head down" and "don't swing too hard" they told me I was "country club ready," which I think was a euphemism for, "I'd like to club you and dump you in the country." I'm sure they were just trying to get rid of me before the school lost any more instructors to tennis or heavy medication.

The day finally arrived when I could pitch Mr. Garner the story of *First Son*. He probably realized what he was in for when he asked what my handicap was and I answered, "I don't speak English too good yet."

We started on the ninth hole of the Bel-Air Country Club. A sadist must have designed this hole, since it has a ravine that's probably 300 to 400 yards wide. You use a rope bridge to cross it and get to the green. Of course, you're supposed to shoot your ball over the ravine first.

If I could picture hell, it would look like the moment I stood on the tee and looked down the fairway. I took my first shot and watched my ball sail into the ravine. I looked at James Garner, smiled sheepishly and put another ball on the tee. That one went looking for my first ball in the ravine. I said one of those curse words I had learned at golf school and addressed another ball, which promptly followed the other two. It was like there was a magnet in the bottom of the ravine (I heard later that the country club members started calling that ravine the Titleist Gap in my honor). After my fifth lost ball, James Garner picked up his ball and said, “Let’s just go to the green.” I think he was trying to put me out of my misery, but it was too late.

When we finally reached the first green, I stood over the ball to putt. Mr. Garner suggested, “Maybe you should read the green.”

“I think I’ll wait for the movie to come out,” I innocently replied.

He shook his head and smiled politely. After a hole or two, between searching for my lost balls in adjacent wildlife preserves and climbing out of bunkers the size of meteor craters, I finally was able to broach the subject of my screenplay. By this point old “Rockford” had figured out I wasn’t Tiger Woods - heck, I wasn’t even Tigger Woods. He also knew that I wasn’t really interested in golfing or saving whales for that matter. Mr. Garner was polite, though, and told me to contact his agent the next time I wanted to pitch him a movie.

I had spent several thousand dollars to better my chances of getting my movie made and all I had to show for it were blisters on my hands and some useless additions to my wardrobe. I could've achieved the same results by doing yard work and had some nice flowers to show for it. My intentions didn't come from the right place, and to be quite honest, the fact that I had given the money to a charity didn't make me feel any better about the situation. Needless to say, *First Son* never got made and the script is still collecting dust somewhere in my basement - right next to my golf clubs.

It wasn't until my wife and I first moved to Branson that I experienced what real charity can do for the soul.

Our flight had been delayed in Dallas and we arrived in Springfield, Missouri at a very late hour. It was so late that the baggage handlers were already losing luggage from the next day's flights. The shuttle busses that ran to Branson had stopped for the evening and we were stranded. There were no cars to rent and not a taxi to be seen anywhere. We were strangers in this part of America and since walking to Branson (which is 35 hilly miles from Springfield) was out of the question, we resigned ourselves to spending the night in the luxurious surroundings of the airport. As I started to create a bed out of our luggage, a woman stopped and asked if we needed a ride. Being from Los Angeles, I looked at her suspiciously. I thought she might be one of those fragile elderly kidnappers known to prey upon foreign-born entertainers. We accepted her offer and she went out of her way to drive us to Branson. When I tried to give her money for gas, she politely refused. She simply said, "Pass on the goodwill." My wife and I were struck by her kindness.

A few years later, I once again arrived at the Springfield airport in the middle of the night because my flight had been delayed. As I was getting into my car I noticed an elderly couple doing a pretty good impression of my wife and I on our inaugural trip to Branson. I stopped to see if they needed any help and they told me they had missed their connecting flight and got separated from their group. The airport was closing and I told them it would be no problem to give them a lift. We enjoyed some polite conversation on the way to Branson and I dropped them off at their hotel. When they offered me gas money I waved them off and told them that I was "passing on the goodwill." The older gentleman had a good sense of humor and replied, "Thanks very much and let me know when you're passing on the good bourbon." I drove away with a great feeling and never mentioned this incident to anyone.

Recently, I was about to do a show for the employees

of the tour line that brings the largest number of customers to my theater. I stood in the wings waiting for the president of this company to introduce me. To my surprise, he told the audience that I was "a great entertainer who picks up complete strangers at the airport and drives them to Branson."

It turned out that the couple I drove to Branson that night happened to be two of his best customers. When the president told the story of my playing taxi driver, the audience erupted in applause. The feeling of warmth that was expressed to me by total strangers was overwhelming and more rewarding than any telethon.

It was the human connection that struck me that evening and I know now that it's the vital ingredient in any act of charity. Even though money given to charity is something that is desperately needed, it's the spirit of goodwill lying behind the donation that's the real gift. I've learned many times in my life that any expression of goodwill has always come back to me at least tenfold and happiness comes from giving without expecting anything in return.

It's like they always say, "True charity is like fruitcake; sooner or later you'll get it back."

A Shot of Smirnoff

The waitress said "If you're driving a Rolls, do you really need a free meal?" I replied, "How do you think I saved enough money to buy the car?"

Chapter 15

Sometimes the Best Dish You Can Eat is Humble Pie

I learned a big lesson from a chance encounter at a Denny's restaurant: (1) always be thankful for what you are blessed with; (2) unless your cholesterol is under 130, a Grand Slam breakfast can't be counted as a blessing; and (3) sometimes the best "free meal" you can get on your birthday is a big helping of humble pie.

It was the late 1980s and my career was humming along quite nicely. I was headlining in Vegas and Atlantic City and making pretty good money. I thought I was hotter than Britney Spears at a navel ring convention. My material success made it easy to forget my days as an amateur struggling to make it in small clubs.

One weekend a friend of mine, Ted Bergman (producer of *Three's Company*, the popular sitcom that was on the air for most of the 1980s), asked my wife and I if we'd like to celebrate my birthday by spending some time at his place in Lake Arrowhead. Lake Arrowhead is a mountain resort community about an hour east of Los Angeles. I asked if Suzanne Somers was part of the deal. "No," Ted said. "But I'll see if I can get Mr. Furley to wear a miniskirt and jump out of your cake." I declined the honor, but did accept Ted's invitation to Lake Arrowhead.

That Friday, my wife, a couple of friends and I got into my "Silver Mink" Rolls Royce and headed toward Ted's house in the mountains (in Beverly Hills, driving a Rolls Royce to a mountain retreat is known as "roughing it"). My stomach began growling because I hadn't eaten all day - I had already finished the last of my wife's Certs and was about to start rummaging between the seat cushions for old French fries. Since we didn't pass anyone else driving a Rolls Royce whom I could ask for Grey Poupon, I was quite relieved when I spotted a sign for a Denny's restaurant.

"Let's go to Denny's," I said. "It's my birthday and I get a free meal." At that time Denny's had a promotion of giving away a free meal if it was your birthday and you had the identification to prove it. Along with learning the Pledge of Allegiance, this is the kind of valuable information that you acquire when you study to become an American citizen. Everybody chuckled as we drove up the ramp to exit the freeway, but little did I know I'd be dining on the "crow" club sandwich that afternoon.

I pulled my Rolls Royce into an oil-stained parking spot in front of Denny's. My car was sandwiched between a rusty Chevy pick-up and a sad-looking '72 Maverick. People stared at the car like it was a silver spaceship instead of your average silver Rolls.

We went into the restaurant and sat at a booth. The waitress dropped off some menus and I asked her about the free meal birthday special.

"Didn't you just drive up in that Rolls Royce?" she asked.

“You bet,” I said grandly.

“And you own it?” she frowned. “If you’re driving a Rolls, do you really need a free meal?”

“How do you think I saved enough money to buy the car?” I replied, trying to be clever and cute. Everyone at our table laughed, but the waitress didn’t think it was very funny. At the time, I was just trying to have a little innocent fun, but when I look back on that day, I can see how insensitive I was. However, my feet would soon be replanted firmly on the ground by the shovel of reality.

After our waitress brought our drinks, I noticed a woman and a young boy seated next to us. The boy was gobbling the food on his plate while the woman watched him, eating nothing herself. I struck up a conversation with her, telling her it was my birthday and I was going to get a free meal. She smiled and said, “It’s my birthday, too.” We all sang “Happy Birthday” to her and were having a good old time until I asked why her son was eating and she wasn’t.

The woman looked at me and explained quietly, “Because I can’t afford a meal.” It was then that I realized she was using her birthday meal to feed her son. My heart broke in that instant. As I looked at her, stupefied, she continued, "It's okay - I'm just so happy my son's getting fed." I could see in her eyes that she really loved that little boy.

I felt ashamed. Here I was, goofing around in a Denny's after driving up in a Rolls and this woman didn't have enough money to buy a roll of Lifesavers. I tried to make up for my insensitivity by offering her my birthday meal, which she graciously accepted. Even though I didn't feel much better about the situation, I was happy that she was going to eat.

I called our waitress over and gave her my credit card. "Put the tab for everyone in the restaurant on my card," I said grandly. "And give yourself a big tip, too." I thought my big "Hollywood" gesture would help me overcome my guilt about the thoughtless way I'd acted. There's a reason Denny's is known for the Grand Slam breakfast - I was about to eat a Grand Slam portion of crow.

After my friends and I finished our meal and got up to leave, an elderly gentleman approached me. "I heard you offered to pay for everyone's meals today," he said. "I'm sorry, but I can't accept."

"Why not?" I said, a little hurt. "There are no strings attached. I just wanted to treat everyone to a free meal."

The gentleman answered, "I appreciate your gesture, but my wife and I've been coming to this restaurant for the past twenty years and Sherry's been our waitress for every dinner. Thank you, but I will pay for my meal and my wife's and leave Sherry her usual tip." He smiled at me and said kindly, "No offense, young man, but the people at this restaurant are my family. You're just a stranger with money." He turned, walked back to his table, pulled out the chair for his wife and they walked away. At the door of the restaurant, he took her hand and held it until they got to their car. It was heartwarming to see such a tender and sincere expression of love.

My friends and I were very quiet as we left the restaurant, got back in the Rolls and continued our trip. That evening had a profound effect on my life. The selfless love that woman showed for her son and the bond between the elderly couple and the waitress were proof that money really is only a tool that we use to get things.

As the Beatles once sang, money can't buy you love and as I learned in Denny's, it won't buy you other important things, like selflessness, self-respect and caring. Luckily for me, what it did buy me that day was some humility and an appreciation for the dignity of others. Those are valuable lessons I intend to never forget.

In my arrogance and insensitivity, I had thought that paying for those people's meals would somehow make their lives better and that they would appreciate my generosity and me. The truth was that they made my life richer, without spending a dime.

A Shot of Smirnoff

In this Soviet Russia the average lifespan was 60 years and the retirement age was 65. It was a great way of getting out of Social Security.

Chapter 16

We're All Going to Kick the Bucket, but We've Got to Keep Kicking Until Then

People talk about intuition and call it a sixth sense. I think there's another one: the sense of purpose in living. I believe it's more important than sight, sound, smell, touch, hearing or intuition. Why?

We can manage without any of the others, but without a sense of purpose, our lives quickly become meaningless.

You hear stories everyday about people who are healthy as a horse until they retire and a month or so later they pass away. They lost their sense of purpose in life, which was all wrapped up in their careers. When their careers ended, so did they.

When I first went to Los Angeles, my parents told me to visit a long-lost relative - the first person in our family to come to America. He was sort of the Christopher Columbus of the Smirnoffs - only he knew the difference between India and America, thank God. My parents described a vibrant, hardworking man whom I pictured as John Wayne with a Russian accent. I remembered as a child listening to the stories about how brave this man was. He came to Los Angeles (which is an act of bravery itself) and forged a future for his family. He was a model for the rest of us. America had Elvis Presley - well, our family had our own Elvis, our hero (only without the rhinestone jumpsuits).

I called his house when I got to Los Angeles and was invited over. I walked into a nicely decorated house and met the family. They were all friendly and excited. I wanted to meet our Elvis; after all, he'd been our inspiration for coming to America - him and the Dallas Cowboy cheerleaders, that is.

When I asked about him, the energy suddenly drained from the room, like when TV evangelist Pat Robertson walks in and starts asking you to confess your sins. Elvis' family told me he was sick, that he'd recently had a stroke. They showed me his room where he lay bedridden and barely able to speak. I'd never met him before, but I felt like I knew him already because of the family stories. Sadly, the man I met was not the hero from those adventures.

The family told me he had been strong as a bull until a month earlier. He had owned and managed convenience stores, but the family had decided to sell the first store he had bought when he arrived in America. That store had been his pride and joy. When they sold the store, two weeks later our Elvis had a stroke. The family realized they'd made a mistake. That store had given Elvis a sense of purpose in his life. No store, no purpose.

In cultures where the elderly are valued, people live much longer. In Russian Georgia, the people live to 120 years old on a consistent basis because they are valued (or at least they looked 120). In American Georgia, they only live to 57 because they sit on the front porch step and the freezer tips over on them. In many Asian countries, they live longer because the people there respect the elderly. In America, old age is treated like a curse. They get about as much respect as a vegetarian at a Texas barbecue.

When I looked down at Elvis, humbled by a stroke, I immediately thought about my parents. In Soviet Russia the average life span was 60 years and the retirement age is 65. It's a great way to get out of paying Social Security, but I realized that my parents could live longer than 60 or 65 if they didn't lose their sense of purpose (or their nitroglycerine pills). So I decided to help them. After all, they had certainly always helped me - they'd been one of the only constants in my life. When I was leaving Russia, they were there. When I was broke, they were there. When I was rich, they were there. When I was getting married, they were there (unfortunately, when I went on my honeymoon, they were there, too). When my children were born, they were there.

I knew that I wanted my parents to be around for a long time and stay healthy, so I bought an apartment building in Los Angeles and asked them to manage it for me. They had a great time living there and were excellent managers. They had a success rate collecting rent that the IRS would envy. Here was their secret: They encouraged tenants to send their children over with the rent checks.

Then they rewarded the kids with candy when they delivered the checks. So the kids bugged their parents for the rent check a week early. Ingenious!

My dad was 89 when he died and my mom ... well, she says she's 29 and who am I to argue? She is healthy and never talks about retiring - she's kind of the Russian version of the Rolling Stones. I don't think about retiring either. Comedians don't retire. Look at Bob Hope ... Rodney Dangerfield ... Strom Thurmond.

Of course, there's nothing wrong with retiring, as long as you can find something else that you love to do. You can change your purpose when you change your job - no one is limited to just one or two purposes in life. So, if you retire or lose your job - and maybe even some of your senses as the body wears out - you still will have a reason to make the most of whatever you have left. After all, if you can make a telephone from two paper cups and a piece of string, anyone can make something great from life no matter what that life looks like.

A Shot of Smirnoff

Sometimes when you get hit between the eyes, the universe follows up with an ice pack to keep the swelling down.

Chapter 17

The Ultimate "Comeback" is Coming Back to Yourself

I have to admit I've led a charmed life in the United States. I have been able to make a living doing what I love - making people laugh. Prior to 1991, I thought that being a comedian was what I did, but the dubious honor of being number one on a David Letterman list helped me discover that being a comedian is who I am.

Before I came to America, I was a comedian in Russia, where I performed on the cruise ships that sailed the Black Sea. My performances consisted of joke telling, dancing and singing. When I arrived in this country in 1977, the only luxury I could afford was a whole new perspective on the differences between life in Russia and America. I figured that I could use my observations as the basis of a new career as an American comedian. So while the U.S. and Russia were building weapons to compete in the arms race, I was building my routine. I became quite successful by pointing out the difference between the two superpowers. For example, in the Soviet Union people line up for hours just to get a tasteless piece of meat and some stale buns; in America you could walk into any fast food restaurant and right away get the same thing.

My style of humor struck a chord with Americans and for a long time my career was hitting nothing but sweet notes. I was regularly turning down ludicrously high-paying jobs in order to stay home with my family. I thought the success I was enjoying as a comedian and actor would last forever, but it all came crashing down in 1991 when the Soviet Union collapsed (my theory is that all the hot air finally escaped). Those inconsiderate politicians - they ended the Cold War without consulting me.

My personal "collapse" came after a commercial break. One evening, I was watching *Late Night with David Letterman* in the comfort of my own bed. For years I had laughed along with the rest of America as Dave went over his Top Ten Lists. That night the topic of Dave's list was "Things that will change immediately now that the Cold War is over." This should be good, I thought. Maybe I'll get some new material for my act. Then Dave announced that coming in at number one (and greeted with laughter from across the nation) was, "Yakov Smirnoff will be out of work."

It's an odd feeling as you watch yourself being given a pink slip on national television. I managed a few chuckles before I turned off the TV. Sure, I thought it was funny, but there was a grain of truth in what Dave had said. The end of the Cold War and the KGB had eliminated 100% of the torture in Russia, 50% of the spying - and 30% of my punch lines. Would the end of communism in Russia really affect my work? Would I end up like Vaughn Meader?

Vaughn Meader was a comedian in the 1960s that had built a very good career doing comic impressions of John F. Kennedy. The night J.F.K. was assassinated Vaughn Meader's career ended. Lenny Bruce, another famous comedian at the time, was booked to perform for a sold-out house in Carnegie Hall the night of Kennedy's assassination. Carnegie Hall's a tough place to perform for anybody, but how could Lenny say anything about the Kennedy tragedy without depressing the audience or seeming disrespectful of JFK? Lenny took the stage and the first thing out of his mouth was, "Looks like Vaughn Meader is screwed!" Apparently the crowd howled - much like they did when Dave Letterman said almost the same thing about me.

After JFK's death, Vaughn Meader's life spiraled out of control and he was eventually arrested on Sunset Boulevard for lewd conduct (and if you've ever seen Sunset Boulevard, you have to be pretty lewd to get arrested there). He never got his career or his life on track after that and eventually ended up in a mental institution.

I was thinking about Vaughn Meader as I tossed and turned in bed that night in 1991. Why had I based so much of my act on the Soviet Union? Why hadn't I diversified my material? That night I watched Leno instead of Letterman.

The next morning I was out getting my mail and my mailman said to me, "Looks like you're out of work, huh?"

"Yeah and I want my unemployment checks delivered to me on time," I joked, trying to be good-natured. The phone rang as I walked back into the house. It was a friend asking if I had seen Letterman. Throughout the day I got calls from dozens of friends and colleagues asking me the same question. I started to panic. Even though it seemed like a harmless little joke, the best humor always contains an element of truth and the truth was that with no Cold War, there was no need for a Cold War comedian. I started getting cold feet and breaking out into a cold sweat when I thought about it. This definitely wasn't funny. The political change meant that most Russians would finally be getting jobs and I would be losing mine. I felt like an East German pole vault manufacturer hearing that the Berlin Wall was coming down. I tried to relax, and just to be on the safe side, began practicing the phrase, "Would you like fries with that?"

It didn't take long for booking agents to follow Letterman's lead. My contracts with casinos in Atlantic City and Vegas were not renewed when they expired, which wasn't good considering my mortgage wasn't even close to expiring. Not only did the entertainment directors of the casinos think I was passé, they were moving away from one-person shows and toward more extravagant entertainments like Siegfried and Roy and Cirque de Soleil. I thought for a second that I could get some exotic animals and learn some magic tricks, but I don't look so hot in leotards.

After my work dried up I thought at the very least I could do the comedy club circuit, but my agent said that nobody wanted to hire me. One day he even let me listen in on a conversation with a club owner who had booked me in the past. I heard the owner say, "Why would I book Yakov? I've got young comics who I don't have to pay as much and they're doing new stuff." After the agent hung up, I said to him, "I guess I don't have to feel guilty about turning down those high-paying gigs to be with my family anymore." I did have a more immediate problem - paying a mortgage that was equivalent to the gross national product of a small country in the South Pacific. Over the next months, I managed to get a few gigs at various clubs for the kind of money that made the free uniform at a fast food joint seem more and more appealing. All the while I was trying to come up with ways to reinvent myself. If I wasn't a Cold War comedian, who was I? A guy with a beard, a funny accent and several commercials to my credit? To add insult to injury, my commercials had also been pulled from TV.

One cold, damp winter night in Rochester, New York, I sat in my hotel room with a comedian friend, Buzz

Nutley, discussing the fact that I had just done a Saturday night show for a grand total of forty people. For a comedian who was used to performing for crowds of over two thousand, it was devastating.

"I need a new hook, something that will bring people in the way my old material did," I told him, "and it has to be something Russian."

Buzz looked at me. "Why?" he asked. "You're a comedian who happens to be Russian, not a Russian who happens to be a comedian."

Boy, talk about getting hit right between the eyes by Mister Obvious! Buzz was right. It was my nature to be a performer, whether I was in Russia, the U.S., or on that island in the South Pacific. I had just happened to be very lucky to come to America during a time of tension between the Soviet Union and the United States. "No problem!" I said to my friend. "I just need to find other things to be funny about."

Sometimes when you get hit between the eyes, the universe follows up with an ice pack to keep the swelling down. A couple of weeks later my agent called and asked me to co-host Farm Aid, the event that Willie Nelson founded to help out farmers who were in dire straits. Since it was a charity event, I wouldn't get paid, but my agent said, "Well, you're getting used to that. Besides, it'll be good for your career."

At that point anything would have been good for my career, but as it turned out, he was right. Appearing at Farm Aid helped me create a whole new life for myself.

The show was in Ames, Iowa. I didn't know what to expect, but I'll never forget the welcome I received from forty thousand people in the middle of America. When I walked out on stage, the crowd went crazy. I thought they must have mistaken me for John Denver, John Mellencamp or perhaps even John Deere. I started by telling them about my first brush with farming. "A friend played a practical joke on me and had me milk his bull," I said. The crowd laughed. Then I added, "I found out that if you milk this animal once you have a friend for life." The crowd roared - and I realized these people didn't watch Letterman! Their response was exactly what I needed. My ego had been starving for quite a while and to me that crowd's laughter and applause was like an all-you-could-eat-buffet at one of those casinos that wouldn't hire me anymore.

When I got off stage, Willie Nelson said, "You should go to Branson, Missouri. They'll eat you up there." I never thought I'd be taking professional advice from Willie Nelson, but since Willie had to declare bankruptcy and nearly went to prison for tax evasion after his manager had embezzled almost everything he owned, I figured he knew how to get out of a hole. I decided I would visit Branson one day, but first I would have to figure out where it was.

Later that month, I was booked at a club in Birmingham, Alabama. I was expecting the worst, but I was delighted - the club was very upscale and successful. I thought the manager of the club would wear overalls and drive a pickup, but he wore an Armani suit and picked me up in a Lexus. He took me out to a leisurely breakfast and then drove me to a newspaper interview. It was unhurried and relaxing, far from the hustle and bustle of Los Angeles. I had a complete sense of peace.

Later that month, my agent booked me on a country talk show called *The Statler Brothers*. I was a little apprehensive about doing a cable talk show, even though it had higher ratings than some of the network late-night talk shows. One of the other guests that night was Shoji Tabuchi, a Japanese fiddler. He had his own theatre in Branson and told me that he packed two thousand people in twice a day. That was the third time something had shown up to point me toward Branson. Now, I may be slow, but I'm not stupid. I decided to take Willie up on his advice.

Branson is a tiny town (population 3,600) situated in the

Ozarks of southwestern Missouri, but it is a major entertainment center, with more theater seats than Broadway and Las Vegas combined. When I first arrived in Branson, I thought, "I can't live here. I've been learning English for 20 years - if I move to the Ozarks, I'd have to start all over again. On the other hand, maybe I could get Dolly Parton to give me a few lessons." Even though I had trouble figuring out that "y'all" meant just me, I found the town quaint and friendly. The people check your hearing all the time - they always say, "Y'all come back now, y'hear?" The first time I went to see Jim Stafford's show in Branson, he invited me up on stage to tell a few jokes. His audience treated me just like the Farm Aid crowd had done. That was all the convincing I needed. I had found my home and an audience with a heart.

To make a long story a little shorter, my family and I moved to Branson. I have my own theater and do sold-out shows for enthusiastic, appreciative audiences. In fact, only in America can a Russian and a Japanese have two of the most popular attractions in Branson (what a country!). Branson has proven to be both a perfect home base for my career and a wonderful place to raise my children. Don't get me wrong, California is great, but I didn't want to bring up my kids in a town where teachers give out gold stars to the student with the most parents at the

PTA meeting.

Instead of following Vaughn Meader's lead and falling into obscurity after the Cold War, my career is now better than ever, but the lessons I learned in 1991 were far more important even than my move to Branson. I learned that no matter what happens in the world - perestroika, glasnost or even being the number one joke on Letterman's Top Ten List - it has nothing to do with who I am. I'm not funny because I'm Russian; I'm just funny. That is my gift, to see things through the eyeglasses of humor. It doesn't matter whether I'm looking at Russia or America or life in general, my gift - such as it is - makes people laugh.

I've learned that one of the secrets to being happy is discovering your gift and having the opportunity to share it with the world, but as I found out, sometimes the universe has to hit you over the head before you realize what you've been given and how to use it in the best way possible. For me, it took being humiliated on national TV and almost going broke, but, as John Deere once said, "Sometimes you have to shovel a lot of manure to raise good crops." Every time I walk out on the stage in Branson, I thank God for the "manure" that brought me to a place where I can share my gifts with my audience.

A Shot of Smirnoff

If someone flips you off on the freeway, you can get upset, or you can say, he thinks I'm number one! Or if you use Viagra and think $10 a pill is a rip off, remember this instead: hey, sixty bucks a year is no big deal.

Chapter 18

"Got Stress? Get Yakov!" 6 Simple Steps to Eliminate Stress

I know that I appear to be your typical, well-balanced, cool-under-fire (although I'm usually shaking in my boots in front of fire), fairly attractive, Russian-American stand-up comic, but believe me, there was a time in my life when I was absolutely falling apart. I was doing three shows a day, writing my first book, trying to be a decent dad to my two kids, negotiating two or three new businesses every day and of course there was my multilevel marketing business (if you'd like to become part of a terrific opportunity for you and your friends, leave your name and I'll be in touch). I was going crazy with a capital N-U-T-S.

A friend who hadn't seen me for a while came over one day and told me I needed to relax. "What gave you a clue I'm stressed?" I asked him. "I dunno - maybe it's the fact that you told the Girl Scout her cookies are lousy." He recommended I try transcendental meditation. I had my misgivings. Who knew what those Maharishi guys would do with my mind once I started meditating? What about my body? I'm too hairy to look good in a loincloth.

My friend said I should meditate for a half-hour every day. "Well, I'm a quick study," I told him. "I'll bet I can do the half-hour in five minutes." He seemed to feel I wasn't taking his suggestion seriously. I assured him I was, took off the fake nose and glasses and then put off the idea of meditation. Anyway, I was much too stressed out to meditate.

A few days later I attended one of those ritzy parties in

Washington D.C., where I ran into an old friend of mine. This friend had a beautiful wife, great kids and a nice home. He knew just about everyone in Washington - he was a real "player," but after a few drinks, my friend looked at me with weary eyes and said, "You know, if I didn't have these parties to go to, I wouldn't have anything." Wow, that sobered me up fast.

We sat together for hours while he poured out his story. It was sad, but also eye opening. I realized that my friend was addicted to approval, recognition and applause. It struck a deep chord. I shuddered as I realized that I was the West Coast version of my friend. I, too, needed the applause. Need it? I couldn't breathe without it. I was addicted to applause and recognition. Back in Russia there was no need for recognition at parties. There was only one party and believe me, you didn't want to be recognized!

For days afterward I thought about my friend. He vividly reminded me that I had to do something about my stress level or it wouldn't be long before the only audience I'd be performing for would be at Dr. Feelgood's Funny Farm for Recovering Comedians. So I decided to give meditation a try. Not just a casual effort - I'd do it the way it was supposed to be done. Amazingly, it worked! My stress level definitely dropped. Of course, within a few months I felt an urge to move to Calcutta and worship cows, but I managed to overcome it.

For me, meditation was a way I could go to an inner place where I could discover the best of myself, where the only one left to impress is me - and that's the one person I can't fool. I found where the real and true reside (and it's not Las Vegas). It's great to be able to throw out all those false faces and make-believe smiles and be honest. Stress became a luxury I could live without. I certainly couldn't live much longer with it.

Meditation helped me develop my own stress management system. It's a six-step approach that I call S.T.R.E.S.S. (easy to remember, huh?) It stands for (1) Stop, (2) Think, (3) Relax, (4) Exercise, (5) Sleep and (6) Strategize. I originally wanted to call it "Yakov Smirnoff's Sure Fire Seventy-Five Simple Steps to Get Rid of Stress, Worry and Anxiety," but nobody could remember a system called Y.S.S.F.S.F.S.S.T.G.R.S.W.A. Heck, I got stressed trying to remember the first two letters - Y.S.!

The S.T.R.E.S.S. system is actually very simple. Whenever you're faced with a stressful situation, the first thing you do is (1) STOP! Most of us react to negative situations by getting stressed. It's an instinctive reaction, kind of like the finger that seems to go up automatically when someone cuts you off on the freeway, but you can't let your first negative reaction control you. If it did, your lifespan might be shorter than a munchkin's inseam. To prevent stress, you need to tell yourself, "STOP!" If you need to, say it out loud. Shout it - "STOP!" If this appears strange to passersby, sing "In the name of love" and do a little dance like Diana Ross and the Supremes. They'll put you away, but you'll get a lot of rest.

The next step is (2) THINK. Take a realistic look at the situation. Understand it for what it truly is and don't blow it out of proportion. Realize that you are in control of the situation, not the other way around. Use your sense of humor. If someone flips you off on the freeway, you can get upset or you can say, "He thinks I'm number one!" If you use Viagra and think $10 a pill is a rip-off, remember this instead: "Hey, sixty bucks a year is not big deal." Finally, ask yourself, "Is this really going to matter ten years from now?" Most of the stuff we get stressed about won't matter ten minutes from now. Life is not what happens to us, life is how we look at what happens to us.

Once you (1) STOP and (2) THINK, the next step is to (3) RELAX. "Wait a minute, Yakov!" I hear you say. "The reason I'm stressed is that I don't have any time to relax!" Believe me, if you don't take the time now, you'll have to take it much sooner than you thought - either at the funny farm or the hospital or, God forbid, the grave. Five minutes spent relaxing can make a lot of difference and a half-hour a day can change your world.

Try doing what compulsive executives do: schedule your relaxation. Put it in your planner (you can call it something else - "executive meeting," "conference call," "performance enhancement," etc. - so everyone will think you're still the same driven son-of-a-gun you've always been). When you do relax, though, relax. Make it a party. Put on a funny hat. Blow up some balloons. Inhale some helium and quack like Donald Duck. Then sit down in a comfortable place. You could even take a bath (here the funny hat is optional). Take the phone off the hook. Give yourself an opportunity to be alone with your thoughts.

You might try meditating, as I do, for 45 minutes every morning. Other people do 20 minutes in the morning, 20 minutes at night. Some super-achievers take five minutes every hour for nine hours. Whatever you do, relaxing regularly in the course of the day can make everything a lot smoother, including you.

The fourth step is (4) EXERCISE. There's nothing better for venting built-up stress than getting out and pounding the pavement or beating the heck out of a punching bag or creaming your opponent in handball or...wait a minute, this was about reducing stress! Whatever you like to do physically to release tension, make sure you schedule it regularly. You can run, walk, ski. Even making love can be terrific for working off stress. I recommend trying for four to five times a week. If you're married...well, skiing is good. The point is, the activity doesn't matter, just get your body moving for at least 40 minutes each time. Again, making love qualifies, and if you're married, you and your wife can use the 35 minutes left over for a nice run.

The next secret is to get enough (5) SLEEP. Eighty percent of all Americans simply don't get enough sleep. Sleep is nature's battery recharge, the Energizer Bunny's best friend. Don't wait until you're speeding down the road at

90 mph to heed your body's call for sleep. Your body knows what it needs - Listen to it! It will speak to you loudly, especially after Mexican food.

The final step is to (6) STRATEGIZE. Create a plan for your life. There's nothing better for reducing stress than knowing where you want to go and how to get there. Without a plan, it's like trying to drive somewhere for the first time without a map (and if you're a guy like me, you'll never stop to ask for directions. Hey, we believe the earth is round, so eventually we'll get there. As long as we're making good time, what's the problem?). When you strategize, you can include time for everything that's important to you, including relaxation. You might even sneak in a vacation or two.

I went to a seminar in Santa Fe where a speaker told us to close our eyes and repeat, "There is nothing I should do." It was a revelation to me about how we let "shoulds" rule our lives. It's programmed into us from childhood - we "should" do our homework, we "should" wash our faces and we "should" pick up our toys. Our lives become a straitjacket of "shoulds" that do nothing but stress us out. I'm suggesting to you that you dump the straightjacket and check yourself out of the "should" funny farm. Do what you choose to do in any moment and tell the "shoulds" to get lost. I guarantee your stress level will stop dramatically in an instant.

So there you have it, Yakov's easy-to-use stress reduction system. All you have to remember is S.T.R.E.S.S. Only don't just remember - do something about it. After all, stress is like in-laws. Everybody has them, but you want to get rid of them as soon as possible.

A Shot of Smirnoff

If my dad was the head of the family, my mother was the neck. The neck turns the head anywhere she wants.

Chapter 19

Stand Up for Yourself- It'll Keep Your Head Above Hot Water

When you see me onstage, I'm not an imposing figure. In fact, part of my appeal is that I'm not threatening. If I were a country, I'd be Liechtenstein - and who's afraid of Liechtenstein? Some people even accuse me of being cute, like that little puppy at the picnic that would never bite anyone. Well, it's true that I've never bit anyone - at least in anger. In fact, I've dodged confrontation like George W. Bush avoiding pretzels. But it took a slug in the head to make me realize that there was nothing cute about being so “nice” when it came to letting others walk all over me.

I never stood up for myself. I accommodated everybody else without question. I trace it back to my childhood - I have turned out just like my father. To say my mom wore the pants in our family was an understatement. If my dad was the head of the family, my mother was the neck and the neck turns the head anywhere she wants. Sometimes my dad ended up with whiplash. My dad’s very nurturing, but he never stood up for himself. What was worse, he never stood up for me, either.

I remember one instance, when I was about ten years old, my mom and dad wanted me to go to summer camp. Now, summer camp is so bad that arts and crafts consist of sewing patches over the holes in your tent. The outhouse doubles as the recreation center. I didn’t want to go, but my dad told me that if I went they would get me the bicycle I had always wanted. I figured I could survive two weeks of just about anything for a bike, so they packed me up and off I went.

Camp Freezeyourbottomoff was miserable - like living at home without the amenities. It was the only place I know of where kids would play Hide and Stay Hidden. The only thing that kept me going was the thought of my new bike. I suffered through two weeks of camp and then finally it was over. I headed home tired, dirty and feeling like a prisoner of war going free and claiming a great prize. Only instead of the beautiful girl next door, my prize would be a shiny new bike (I was only 10 years old, remember - I had different priorities back then).

My proud parents picked me up and pumped me for news on how camp went and what I had learned. "Great!" I said. "Here - I made you an ashtray with the microphone already built in. Now, what about my bike?"

We talked for a while longer, but every time I brought up the bike, my mom changed the subject. Finally, when we got home, I asked point blank, "When am I going to get my new bike?"

The silence was deafening - like listening to a mime on the radio. I remember my mom standing at the ironing board with her back to me. That's when she dropped the bombshell - there would be no bike. "It's too dangerous," she said. Dangerous? It wasn't as if I intended to use it to jump the fountain in front of the Kremlin, but my parents had always treated me, their only child, with kid gloves. They didn't want me riding around on a bike. They lied to me and not for the last time, either - I believed in Santa Claus until I was 23.

It wasn't fair. I had held up my end of the bargain by suffering, through two weeks at Camp Freezeyourbottomoff. Now they were backing out of our deal. I argued with my mom for what seemed like forever and I looked to my dad to support me, but he didn't take my side. He just sat there silently, letting my mother do all the talking. I remember watching my father, feeling his helplessness and somehow believing that this must be acceptable behavior for a man.

After the saga of the missing bike, I learned to avoid conflict at all times, just like my dad. I didn't realize the price of that choice until I got clobbered on TV - literally - even though it wasn't in the script. I was a guest star several times on the 1980s TV series *Night Court*, which starred magician and comedian Harry Anderson. I played an immigrant (I know, what a stretch). I greatly appreciated the opportunity because I loved working with everyone on that show. I assumed everyone liked working with me, too. Not!

One day the whole cast was assembled to run through a particular scene. I was standing right next to "Bull", a character played by Richard Moll, who is 6'6" (I, on the other hand, wear lifts in my shoes to get on the Space Mountain ride at Disneyland). All of a sudden Bull turned around and punched me in the head. I flew across the room like gravity had been suspended and landed somewhere off the set. I traveled so far, I thought I had jet lag when I came to.

Everyone gathered around to see if I was okay. I was waiting to see if I was all right myself. Why did Bull hit me? Maybe he identified with Bullwinkle and my accent reminded him of Boris and Natasha. One minute he was totally calm, the next he belted me. I remember feeling more confused than mad (believe me, with an opponent as big as Richard Moll, it's better to be confused than mad). But Harry Anderson was mad. He called Bull several names that I can't put in this book and then said, "Let's you and me go outside and you can fight someone your own size." Of course, that would have meant going into the woods and finding a grizzly bear.

Harry was a big man - more important, he was a much bigger star than Bull. The tension on the set was rising. Fearing a lawsuit, executives from Warner Brothers came running. They stepped in front of Harry and asked Bull to apologize to me. They even organized a dinner for the entire cast and me, where Bull stood up and publicly apologized to me and I accepted. I guess they thought that the dinner would cost less than a lawsuit.

For me, that interchange was a revelation. For the first time in my life, someone had stood up for me. That was great, of course, but why hadn't I stood up for myself? Suddenly, late in life, I had learned a lesson I should have learned as a child. I had to start standing up for myself. I thought the first thing I had to do was go back to my mother and ask for the bike she had promised me, but I realized I'd look silly riding down the streets of Hollywood with training wheels. It wasn't too much later, though, I put the lessons of standing up for myself to use in a much more important arena.

In 1996 I moved from Los Angeles to Branson, Missouri and opened my own theater. At first it was difficult - not just getting people to come to my shows, but simply to learn to speak hillbilly. I tried everything to drum up business. I attended other performers' shows and mingled with the audiences. I went to local hotels at breakfast time and chatted to the patrons. I entertained representatives from the tour companies that bring lots of customers to Branson. You name it, I did it - anything to make the show a success. I even learned to eat grits.

It wasn't easy, but after three long years, the crowds slowly started filling my theater. I was relieved because (1) I was getting tired of grits and (2) now I could concentrate on the show and let someone else handle the management of the theater and public relations. I hired a theater manager, a gung-ho guy from the East Coast. He drove right into town and took over the company. "If you want me to help you, I need to be the boss. You've got to get out of the way and let me run things," he said. I agreed and he began an aggressive marketing campaign while I focused all my attention on my comedy act and producing the show. The manager erected Yakov Smirnoff billboards all over town. He produced radio spots. He even ordered the giant statues of me. While this was going on, I was happily doing what I do best - performing. A lot of performers fall into this trap. We only want to do what we love and we're delighted to leave the business side of our careers to someone else. Unfortunately, like Martha Stewart's version of homemade moonshine, that's a recipe for disaster. We learn that life is like school: you can't play around forever if you want to make the grade.

For two years, it seemed things were going great. The theater was full, it looked like we were successful and I left the business details to the manager. We even became very good friends. I was taken with his energy and decisiveness. I soon learned that it's easy to be decisive when it's somebody else's money, but this man also kept me completely separate from everything having to do with the running of my theater.

Then inconsistencies started showing up. The audiences at my theater started shrinking - 700, then 600, then 500 per show. When I asked the manager about it, he replied, "Hey, business sucks" and promised to get right on it. He ordered more billboards (that seemed to be his answer to everything: more billboards). I already had 80 percent of the billboards in town, so soon I had 90 percent. Even I got sick of seeing my picture everywhere. I wouldn't have been surprised to see my face under a Smokey the Bear hat saying, "Only you can prevent forest fires!"

The attendance at my shows picked up a little, just enough to stop my worrying and pay for the cost of the extra billboards. But in truth, I simply didn't think about it. What I didn't know couldn't hurt me, could it?

I found out how wrong I was. I was attending the Andy Williams Christmas party with a friend, Arno Wehr. I noticed people were avoiding me as if I'd forgotten my deodorant. Nobody would talk to me - and by that time, I did know how to speak hillbilly. Finally, Arno, who owns Tribesman Resort in Branson, pulled me aside and said, "Yakov, do you have any idea what's going on with your theater? Do you know how much money you owe people?"

"No," I said, "That's the manager's department."

Arno pointed to the crowd and said, "Well, you may not know how much you owe, but they do."

A chill ran down my spine. I went back to the office and checked the books for the first time in years. I found out why I wasn't exactly the life of that party - there was more red in the ledgers than I had seen since I left Communist Russia. I was over a million dollars in debt! I owed almost everybody in town. Needless to say, I didn't have enough petty cash to cover these bills. I went to bed that night, but instead of dreaming the American dream, I tossed and turned in the American nightmare of too much debt and too little cash.

The next day, in a panic, I called Terri Tucker, a business consultant I knew. What she said to me completely turned me around. She asked, "Yakov, what is it that your manager does that you can't do for yourself?" At that moment I had a vision of my mom standing at the ironing board back in Russia. Only this time, she turned toward me and said, "Go get 'em, Tiger!" So for the first time in my life, I stood up for myself. I confronted my manager about what was going on. I was nervous, sweating like a freshman asking the head cheerleader to the high school prom and hoping her football-jock boyfriend wasn't around. The manager confirmed my worst fears about the amount of debt. "In that case, " I said, "you have to go." He replied that he hadn't paid himself for six months. Either I should pay him his back salary or he proposed to stay on until he got paid. That wasn't a workable solution as far as I was concerned (talk about leaving the fox in charge of the hen house!), so I managed to scrape together enough money to pay him off.

My accountant recommended I file for bankruptcy, but I refused to do that. It took me two days to get up the nerve and I had to swallow my pride (luckily by that time I didn't have a lot left, so it was a small meal). Finally I sat down at my desk, took out my personal phone book and started calling my creditors. I told them I wanted to pay them in full and intended to do so, but they would need to wait. Needless to say, at that point I was about as popular in Branson as Jesse Helms at an ACLU rally. After the last phone call, the fax machine rang and out popped a cartoon with a guy on a horse, hanging over a cliff, with a crowd of people holding onto a rope that kept him from plunging over. The caption read, "Hang on, Yakov, people will help." That cartoon brought tears to my face and warmth to my heart.

The next day the phone started ringing. Most of my creditors offered to forgive part of my debt with them. Rather than being angry, they seemed excited that I was finally standing up for myself. They were happy to be in direct contact with me instead of dealing with my former manager. Eventually I paid back every single dollar of my debts and my relationships with the people of Branson are excellent. I have a very capable administrative team in place, but I'm the one responsible for my career and business. I've learned the value of asking for what I want and standing up for myself. I know no punch can knock me out because I'm grounded in what I know is right for me.

A Shot of Smirnoff

Refugee camp was noisy, dirty and no one spoke English - perfect training for moving to New York City. Part of the immigration process required us to be interviewed by the authorities to make sure we weren't Communists, spies or even worse - telemarketers.

Chapter 20

"Fill Your Well" with Love - You Never Know When Someone Will Need A Drink

Sometimes the most poignant lessons in life are learned while enduring the most pain. Frying bacon in the nude can teach you that basic concept. My friend Gregory taught me a simple yet powerful lesson that has become a cornerstone of my life - love yourself first. It might seem like a rather selfish act, considering most traditional religions and conventional wisdom tells us to give our love to others. However, I have come to believe that without loving yourself first, it is impossible to accept love from others, much less give your own love away.

It was 1977 when I first met Gregory. My parents and I were living in a refugee camp in Italy after leaving communist Russia. It was noisy, dirty and no one spoke English - perfect training for moving to New York City. Part of the immigration process required us to be interviewed by the authorities that made sure we were not Communists, spies or - even worse - telemarketers, before allowing us to continue on to our destination - America.

Gregory was unlike any Russian I had ever known (in other words, he was sober). He was a handsome, charismatic man who could charm his way into any woman's heart, body or soul and not necessarily in that order. Since I was a naive young man who had lived with his parents for the first 26 years of my life, I wanted desperately to learn the secrets of Gregory's success.

What really drew me to Gregory was his incredible and daring sense of humor. He would do almost anything to get a laugh - he was like a comedy club without the two-drink minimum. I was envious of his bravado, not to mention the many women he would cast his spell upon. We spent a couple of months together in the Italian camp and by the time we were cleared to travel to America, Gregory and I had become the Russian version of *Dumb and Dumber*. I thought Gregory was the luckiest guy in the world and I'd lie awake at night thinking of how I could become more like him.

Gregory loved a practical joke, even if it involved a little pain. For example, my parents and I finally arrived in New York and after settling in, I called Gregory and made a date to get together. I met Gregory at a Chinese restaurant where he proceeded to eat an entire spoonful of hot mustard. He told me it was a delicacy. Soon Gregory's eyes began to water. I asked him why he was crying and he told me that when he was a little boy he had gone swimming with his friend and his friend had drowned. Then he offered me a huge spoonful of the mustard. I gulped it down, thinking it was an appetizer and my own eyes began tearing up like Halle Berry getting an Oscar. As I signaled the waiter for water, Gregory laughed and asked why I was crying. I said, "I feel badly that your friend drowned instead of you!"

One night I confessed to Gregory that I was afraid to do stand-up comedy in America. Gregory promised that he would help me. Since I had only been in my new country a short time, my English was a combination of Arnold Schwarzenegger's accent and Sylvester Stallone's mumble - perfect for an action film star, but not so great for a comedian. Over the next few weeks, Gregory tutored me while he translated my Russian material for American audiences. Without his help and encouragement, I don't think I would ever have been able to perform in the United States.

In order to get professional work, comedians showcase their talent for comedy club owners - five-minute performances in front of the toughest possible audience. It can be the longest five minutes of any comedian's career, longer than waiting for a contractor to finish renovating your bathroom. My first showcase set was at Catch a Rising Star in New York.

The night of my first showcase, Gregory knocked on my door and we headed out for the comedy club together. I noticed Gregory acting more strangely than usual while we rode the train to our destination. When I asked him what was going on, he told me he had tried smoking some marijuana with his neighbor. Gregory would try anything and I just shrugged it off as "youthful indiscretion" (That excuse works for most American politicians, so why not for Gregory?).

My performance at the comedy club went well and over the next few weeks, I worked hard to hone my comedy routine. Gregory helped when he could, but I noticed that he was drinking a lot more and partying even harder. He never had a shortage of women, either. He was like a Russian version of Teddy Kennedy. Gregory got more girls by accident than I ever got on purpose (although whenever I got the girl, it was usually by accident, too).

Gregory could be the most helpful, caring guy in the world, but then would turn around and try and steal my girlfriends - and he was successful on more than one occasion. So when I began dating my wife-to-be, I refused to introduce her to him. I planned on keeping this one for myself! When Gregory asked about her I showed him a picture of one of my aunts and said proudly, "That's my Linda! And she'll be even more beautiful after the dental work and facial electrolysis." After that, he stopped asking about her.

After I moved to Los Angeles, I became a regular performer at The Comedy Store on Sunset Boulevard. Gregory had also moved out to the West Coast and we remained friends. I introduced him to Mitzy Shore, who owned and ran The Comedy Store. Mitzy had become a friend and a business acquaintance and it wasn't long before Gregory began trying to charm her. I took Gregory aside and asked him as a friend to lay off because I didn't want anything to jeopardize my relationship with Mitzy. At this point in my career I couldn't afford to pay a toll fee, let alone an entire bridge. Gregory flashed his devilish smile and said, "We'll see," but he didn't back off and I didn't appreciate him ignoring my request. Our relationship cooled after that and I didn't speak to him for several months.

However, I missed my friend and it was pretty easy to forgive him. I tried calling him, only to find that his telephone had been disconnected. Letters I sent were returned marked, "not at this address." I even took out ads in the newspapers to try and find him.

Mitzy often asked me if I had heard from Gregory and I would just smile and shrug. I thought of him often over the next couple of years and wondered what new adventures he was having. Whenever I saw a dapper gentleman on the street or looked down at the hot mustard in any Chinese restaurant, memories of my friend sprang to mind. I figured that Gregory was out doing what he did best, charming the ladies and leading a life of variety and intrigue.

A couple of years later I received a call from a doctor in New York. Gregory was in the hospital. I immediately flew to the Big Apple to be with my friend. When I walked into his room, however, I was shocked and saddened by what I saw. He looked more like death itself than the handsome, masculine man I once knew. His eyes were sunken, his skin was pasty and his body a mere whisper of what it once had been. I hesitated to walk to his bedside, but Gregory managed a smile and said, "Don't worry, old friend. Hot mustard is not on the menu in this hospital." We shared a good laugh, which momentarily kept me from weeping. I adjusted his pillow to try and make him comfortable.

"Better?" I asked.

"Now that you are here, yes." He told me I was the only one who came to see him. I stared at him for a moment, searching my empty head for something to say. Then Gregory broke the silence. "Do you have friends Yakov, real friends?"

"Yes, of course," I answered, "and you're one of them."

Gregory smiled. I looked down at this man who I once envied. The things that had brought Gregory pleasure - drinking, drugs, philandering - were now the very things destroying him. Our times together flashed before my eyes. I thought about how we had been friends for so long, but he had never really expressed his feelings for me. I realized that his relationships with women had also been superficial, lasting about as long as cold beer on a hot day.

My envy turned to compassion. I smiled softly at my ailing friend and told him that I loved him. He smiled back as a tear crawled from the corner of his eye and ran down his cheek. Then he told me a joke. "Yakov, here's one for your act. The little ant got married to a female elephant. Only after the wedding night, the elephant died. When his friends came to visit the ant, they found him distraught. 'You must have loved her a lot,' they said. 'Sure,' he replied. 'But that's not why I'm crying. I'm crying because for one night I enjoyed myself - and now, for the rest of my life, I have to dig this grave.'"

I laughed through my tears. Gregory took a deep raspy breath. Mustering all his remaining strength, he whispered, "Yakov, remember this. When your well is empty, you can't give water to a thirsty man."

Gregory began to cough uncontrollably, his gasps for breath bringing in the nurses who asked me to leave.

Two days later, he was gone. I often thought about

what his last words meant. Gregory had whispered, "When your well is empty, you can't give water to a thirsty man," which, simply put, means you can't give anything away you don't have. He was saying that if you don't love yourself, it's impossible to share your love with anybody else. Something buried in Gregory's psyche wouldn't allow him to love himself. Even on his deathbed he was trying to help me, a successful comedian, by giving me stuff for my act, but he never learned how to receive love. He tried in vain to fill the void inside with wine, women and song. The wild lifestyle became his pacifier.

I felt a new understanding deep inside. Suddenly, my friend's empty life and lonely death had become a powerful lesson for me. Gregory gave me what I needed to re-chart my course toward true happiness by learning to love myself first.

W.H. Auden said, "We must love one another or die."

Steven Stills wrote, "Love the one you're with."

I say, "Love yourself first and fill your well." There are a lot of thirsty people out there, so you need to be ready to give them a drink.

A Shot of Smirnoff

Great! First I can't find a babysitter in all of Missouri, and now I don't need one because I can't find my kids.

Chapter 21

"Discovering the Greatest Gift: The "Present"

Not too long ago my 401 (k) shrank to a 34 (b). What we don't seem to realize is that the future occupies neither time nor space and therefore doesn't actually exist. So when people tell you that you have no future, you can just smile and agree with them. What I really mean is that in our never-ending quest to control our destiny, sometimes we forget that the moment we're in right now is so much more important than the moments we envision off on the distant horizon.

I bet after Neil Armstrong had accomplished the unimaginable by landing on the moon, somebody asked him, "So, what's next, Neil?" He probably replied, "I just got back from the moon! How about a shower that doesn't involve meteors for a change?" While it's important to plan ahead, it's equally important to be aware of and enjoy the moment we're in.

I found this out the hard way in 1996. My wife was out of town for a few days and I had to play Mr. Mom to Natasha, age 6 and Alexander, age 4. To be honest I was a little nervous about not having my wife around, but I was grateful the kids weren't still breast-feeding. For a treat I wanted to take my kids to a place called Silver Dollar City, kind of like a Six Flags Over the Ozarks theme park. It is only a few miles from Branson. It has rides, a petting zoo and a booth where they teach you family crafts, like milking a cow.

We were just stepping out the door when the phone rang. It was a friend calling to invite me to a parenting seminar later that afternoon. I had signed up for the seminar several weeks earlier and a spot had finally opened up. I really wanted to attend, but it was an adults-only event (I suppose they didn't want a bunch of kids shouting out objections during the seminar). If I wanted to go, I would have to rustle up a babysitter.

I quickly made some phone calls to find someone who could look after the kids when we returned from our morning at the amusement park. However, babysitters seem to have an uncanny ability to avoid your calls when you really need them. I left my cell number on a few answering machines and the kids and I took off for Silver Dollar City. Normally the park is only a half-hour drive from our home, but as luck would have it, we immediately got stuck in traffic on the way out of town. I sat there in stony silence, worrying about when the road would clear, how I could make sure the kids had a good time and how I was going to get back in time for the seminar.

My daughter, Natasha, asked when we'd get there.

"Soon," I said.

We slowly moved a few miles and she asked again.

"Soon," I repeated.

"Daddy, we passed 'soon' five minutes ago," she said.

"I know, but we're getting close to 'almost there,'" I replied.

In the mean time, my son, Alexander, sat patiently in the back seat enjoying every minute of the anticipation.

The traffic finally cleared up and we made it to the park. I tried to get both the kids on the roller coaster, which was fine with my daughter who's keen to try anything at least ten times, but my son is two years younger and understandably a little more timid. So we opted for a carousel ride that both children were happy with.

As my children were jumping onto the carousel, I was jumping all over the buttons on my cell phone trying to track down a babysitter. Just then a stranger told me my kids were adorable. I smiled politely while dialing yet another potential sitter's number. My kids spun around the carousel while my head spun with other possible solutions. More teenage girls rejected me that day than all my years in high school. It was so difficult to find a sitter I thought I'd better check the newspaper to see if there was an 'N Sync concert in town. In my preoccupation with my desires, I didn't realize how "out of sync" my priorities were that day.

Suddenly, my phone rang. I hoped it was finally some good news and I ducked around the corner to get away from the banjo music to take the call. Much to my dismay, it was another rejection. I went back to the carousel ride and received an even greater shock - my children were nowhere to be found.

Just before panic set in I thought, "Great! First, I can't find a babysitter in all of Missouri and now I don't need one because I can't find my kids." While I scoured the area, looking among the other parents and children for my son and daughter, I realized that I had done the worst thing a parent can do - lose his children. My Father of the Year award would have to wait for another year. I was trying to picture how I would explain this to my wife. "Honey, I've got good news and bad news. The good news is the kids had a great time at Silver Dollar City. The bad news is they're still having a great time at Silver Dollar City."

I searched the park frantically. I asked dozens of attendants, "Have you seen my kids?" It must have seemed like a ridiculous question to them, given there were thousands of kids at the park that day. The search seemed to go on forever, longer even than it takes for your bags to show up on the airport baggage carousel. It was probably only a few minutes before Natasha and Alexander rushed to my side, but they were both out of breath and my son's face was filled with pride. "Daddy, Daddy, I rode the roller coaster and I wasn't afraid! Did you see me, did you, did you?"

"Don't ever run off like that again," I snapped. Instantly, my joy turned to tears. My daughter stared at me in disbelief. My panic and anger had destroyed my children's excitement. This was no Kodak moment. It was more like a Kojak moment.

Despite the children's attempts to enjoy the rest of the afternoon, I continued to be preoccupied by my desire to find a sitter. The drive home was like an uncomfortable date. Nobody spoke. I had the radio turned on low, but even Rush Limbaugh on the radio seemed afraid to break the tension. When I got home, I checked my answering machine: no messages. It was hopeless - I was going to miss the seminar.

I was in a funk while I made the kids dinner. My son was playing with his food so I set a timer and told him that if he didn't finish up in five minutes, there would be no story that night. He started eating faster and only had two mouthfuls left when the timer went off. Normally, I would have said that was all right, but I was frustrated so I said, "That's it! No story tonight."

He cried and ran to his room. His sister protested in his defense, "Dad, that wasn't fair." Then she ran to her room. I sat there alone, wondering what had gone wrong. I just wanted to be a good parent - after all, that's why I so desperately wanted to attend the seminar.

I sat on the sofa trying to relax when I looked up. Both of my children were peeking at me from behind the door. In a stern voice I said, "What is it now?"

They ran over to the couch and threw themselves on me. Hugging me, they said, "We love you, daddy. We just wanted to say goodnight."

They curled up in my arms while I choked back my tears. I told them how sorry I was and that I was immersed in "adult things." I hadn't been their friend, and it destroyed me inside to realize how out of whack my priorities had been that day.

Long after I had tucked my kids in, I returned to their bedrooms and watched them sleeping. I felt so blessed to have two beautiful, healthy children. I realized then that I hadn't missed out on a seminar that day. I'd attended the parenting class anyone could participate in, taught by my own children. Unfortunately, that day I had flunked the test. For five hours that afternoon my kids had been enjoying themselves, despite a father who was elsewhere in mind and spirit. I'd been so focused on making something happen in the future that I had missed what was happening in the present. Incredibly, what I had missed was the very thing I had hoped to learn in the seminar - how to be a better parent.

I've applied the simple lesson that I learned from my children that day to other aspects of my life and it's been one of the greatest gifts I've ever received. I realized that you couldn't give the past to someone because it's already gone. You can't give someone the future because it isn't here yet. The only time you can give and experience happiness is right now. That's why we call it the present.

Give It

"Share the Wealth" Doesn't Mean "Stick 'Em Up"

A Shot of Smirnoff

I replaced the previous bartender who was an American Indian. He got fired because every time somebody ordered a Manhattan he charged twenty four dollars.

Chapter 22

To Get a Helping Hand, You'd Better Stick Out Your Own

One of the most valuable lessons I have learned in America is, "People will help you if you're willing to help yourself." I was working as a bartender at Grossinger's Hotel when I first met the man who would help me immensely in my career. Grossinger's was nestled in the Catskill Mountains a couple of hours north of New York City. The hotels there were famous for the comedians and entertainers who preformed on their stages from the 1950s to the 1990s. I took the job to learn about show business in America while I made a living pouring drinks for the patrons. I replaced the last bartender, who was an American Indian. He got fired because every time somebody ordered a Manhattan he charged twenty-four dollars.

The head bartender (and my boss) was a portly Greek fellow named Paul, a gruff man with curly black hair and a face that had little chance of ever forming wrinkles from smiling too much. He said very few words to me, which really didn't help my English, but I did learn to grunt in Greek.

One evening the featured act in the bar lounge was a group of Russian dancers and singers. As we stood behind the bar and watched them entertain the enthusiastic audience, Paul turned to me and asked if I could dance and sing like that. I told him that I was a comedian in Russia and could sing and dance and make people laugh while I did it. I'm sure it didn't come out quite right, but Paul grumbled something about giving me a shot. He said, "Heck, if they can do it, why not you?" Listening "between the grumbles," I could sense that Paul was encouraging me and I felt empowered to take the initiative to make something happen.

The next day, I found out that the entertainment director was going to be conducting a game of Simon Says at the hotel. At the time, my act consisted of a few jokes and a dance number where I would take off my street clothing to reveal a Russian outfit underneath. I went to see Jerry Weis, the man who booked the talent and boldly asked him if I could perform as the opening act for the afternoon activities.

"What do you do?" he asked.

In broken English I said, "I take my clothes off and people laugh."

I'm not sure what he expected, but he was intrigued enough to give me a chance to perform. I prepared for my big break like Susan Lucci preparing a daytime Emmy acceptance speech. I practiced my dancing and recited a few jokes to myself in the mirror. The big day came and I felt ready to do my thing.

It was an older audience and I imagined the Simon Says game would go something like, "Simon says, restart your pacemaker." The emcee introduced me and I began my routine. I was quite nervous and the audience didn't really know how to react at first, but I kept a smile on my face and kept plugging away. After a couple of very long seconds, people started laughing. Then something happened that I had never experienced before in my career as a comedian - a woman in the audience began laughing like a hyena. After I made a few comments about her very loud response, she laughed even harder - until two ambulance attendants entered and placed her on a gurney. It might sound like I'm making this up, but the poor woman was actually having a seizure in the middle of my act.

Right after I finished my comedy, people came over and said that I was "killing." I said, "I didn't mean to." At the same time, out of the corner of my eye, I noticed a young man at the back of the room. When he saw me looking at him, he quickly ducked behind a pillar.

That night when I went back to work in the bar, Paul told me that the mysterious young man was Mark Addis, the nephew of the hotel's owner. Mark worked at the hotel, too, but since he was related to the owner he was part of the "royal family" and I was just a lowly servant. While I was at Grossinger's we went to many of the same parties, but since I was working, we never had any contact. After about six months, I moved to Los Angeles and never really gave Mark another thought.

Several years later when my career had begun to take off, I received an exciting phone call from my agent. I had been booked to headline at the Trump Plaza Hotel in Atlantic City. Headlining the big rooms at the casinos is important for comedians. The money is very good, the prestige is incredible and, of course, there are the free buffets. When I arrived at the hotel, who should greet me but Mark Addis! Even though he wasn't hiding behind a pillar this time, I knew who he was. He told me that he had seen me on *The Tonight Show* and thought I was great. Mark was responsible for giving me the opportunity to headline at Trump Plaza, an important entry for me in the world of big-time entertainment.

Mark handed me keys to a luxury suite. I said, "I'll have it cleaned in half an hour." But he said the suite was for me and told me I had carte blanche at the hotel. I said, "Who is Blanche and where do I have to cart her?"

"No," he explained, everything was paid for and that I could just toss the key behind me and close the door at the end of the week. This was a bachelor's dream come true. My shows went very well and it was Mark who made the calls to his friends in Las Vegas and got me booked into the big rooms there. I enjoyed many great years working in Las Vegas, the only city in the world where you can lose your shirt and get a tan at the same time.

Over the years Mark and I became great friends and I looked forward to his company as much as I did the work he gave me. The enthusiasm that he exuded was electric and touched everyone who came into contact with him. We often talked about the days at Grossinger's. Once I asked him what he had thought about a comedian who hardly spoke English. "Yakov, the first time I saw you I knew by the look in your eyes that you had a dream and there was nothing in the world you would rather be doing than making people laugh," he told me. "I also know your motivation is to give something of value to people. I wanted to help you because you were working so hard to help yourself." I thought, if he could tell all that by looking in my eyes, no wonder I stink at poker and he runs the casino.

Even though we were both very busy (I went on to

become a successful comedian and Mark became Donald Trump's right-hand man) we managed to stay in touch. It was Mark Addis who built the Taj Mahal Resort and Casino in Atlantic City (well, Mark and several hundred-construction workers, that is). It was obvious to me that the hardest working man in show business was not James Brown, but Mark Addis. I really respected him for the way he handled his professional and his personal life.

One day I was driving on the freeway in Los Angeles when I received a call on my cell phone. My agent told me he had to give me some bad news. Mark Addis had just died in a helicopter crash. I pulled over to the side of the road and sobbed. I couldn't believe that my friend was dead. I remembered all the times we'd enjoyed together, how his eyes twinkled with the look of a man doing exactly what he absolutely loved to do. He crammed several lifetimes worth of achievements into a very brief stay on earth. He was a good friend and I am very sad that he is gone.

It wasn't long after Mark's passing that my career took a downturn. When the Soviet Union fell, my bank account followed. After a few years of learning to reuse teabags and really appreciate the blue light specials at K-Mart, I moved to Branson and got my theater off the ground. In the next three years, I worked really hard to put people in seats - harder than the head shredder at Enron. Even though at times I felt discouraged, I remembered what Mark had said about helping me because I helped myself. So I put my nose to the grindstone and pushed harder. Boy, did that hurt! I wish someone had clued me in that it was only an expression.

Then a unique opportunity presented itself. I was booked to perform for the National Tour Association convention in Atlantic City. The association was made up of tour operators who could potentially produce up to 50 percent of my future revenue by bringing motor coach tour groups to my show. They could make the Yakov Smirnoff Theater a prominent landmark on the Branson map (up until that time, my theater was more like a rest stop).

It was very difficult to get this particular showcase, but my agent, Robert Williams, did everything in his power to make it happen. The show was in Atlantic City at the Taj Mahal Hotel. There were 2,500 people crammed into the room and I knew how important this particular night was for the future of my theater. That night I performed one of the best shows of my life. When

I took my final bow, 2,500 tour operators gave me a standing ovation.

As I lifted my head, I looked to the back of the room where a large neon sign flashed in brilliant colors. It said, "The Mark Addis Arena." I shivered with understanding. I had worked extremely hard and I believe Mark was watching me. It wasn't just the electric company that lit up that sign. Mark was there for me again, helping out somebody who was helping himself.

A Shot of Smirnoff

Since both the US and the USSR had vastly different political ideologies, the two diplomats would sit in a room for days and not even speak with each other. It was like they had been married for 45 years.

Chapter 23

Sometimes the Best Bridge is Laughter

I am a court jester. My calling in life is to make people laugh. I used to worry that perhaps being a professional comedian didn't bring much value to the world, since the reaction to a joke comes and goes, there doesn't seem to be anything tangible left behind. Some of my childhood friends have become engineers, doctors and teachers. An engineer eventually sees his bridge being built. A doctor sees his patients get well (unless the HMO has something to say about it). A teacher sees her students learn and grow. All a comedian sees, if he's lucky, is a laughing, applauding audience that, at least for a while, has forgotten its cares and problems. But, is that all there is to it?

I don't think like that anymore. Scientists have proven that laughing is like "internal jogging" that exercises your heart muscle along with your "heart," helps build lung capacity and releases endorphins - the chemicals that trigger pleasure sensations in the brain. We can only think one thought at a time. When you're laughing, you know it's a happy thought. Try laughing and thinking of an IRS audit at the same time. It doesn't work!

All the evidence points to humor and laughter being much needed facts of our lives. Everybody's heard the line, "Laughter is the best medicine" (which is true unless you're suffering from a hangover, then maybe an Alka-Seltzer might be more appropriate). The question that concerned me was this: Is being a comedian significant enough to make a difference to society on a large scale? I just wasn't sure.

A visit to what remains of the ancient city of Pompeii in Italy set me thinking. Pompeii was a favorite resort where wealthy Romans would holiday back in the really, really, really old days. It was completely destroyed when Mount Vesuvius erupted in 79 A.D. The volcanic blast engulfed all the buildings and statues in ash and cinders. It looked like Los Angeles the day after the Lakers won an NBA championship.

All of the statues were destroyed except one - only the statue of the court jester survived. In those days, court jesters delivered news to the emperor (just like today's local TV anchors - except jesters were trying to be funny). If the news was particularly bad, the jester used humor to lighten the blow. If the jester could make the emperor laugh and forget his troubles, then the jester had done his job and could go on living among royalty. If the jester wasn't very amusing, he would often be condemned to death - the ultimate in immediate job performance feedback. Luckily, nowadays if a comedian "dies" it just means they'll probably lose their sitcom development deal at Fox.

Since statues had been built to honor the jesters, I realized that they must have been considered important people and their work had been valued. It wasn't until 1984 that I had the opportunity to experience this in my own career. It was then that I saw humor change the world.

It started when I met President Ronald Reagan. After a show at a Washington D.C. comedy club, a man named Arno came up and introduced himself to me. Arno was a major power broker in the D.C. area and he told me he was holding a small dinner party for President Reagan and the First Lady. He said he wanted me to attend the party and that he would introduce me to the Reagan's.

A few weeks later I flew back to Washington for the party. Arno picked me up at the airport and we drove back to his house. There were military helicopters hovering over the area with searchlights so powerful I needed SPF 30 sun block. The Secret Service had secured four city blocks surrounding the house. My first thought was 'They're not being very secretive.' We pulled up to the driveway and the Secret Service checked our identification. My host gave the agent his I.D. and was asked if he had another form of identification. As he handed over another card, the agent looked it over suspiciously. He finally gave the host of the party the thumbs up, then looked across at me, smiled, and said, "Hey, I saw you on the Miller Lite commercial, you're hilarious. Come on in." As we entered the house, I was reminded once again that it's sometimes easier to open doors with humor than with power.

So, incredibly, there I was, sharing this lavish dinner table with an elite group of 18 dignitaries from all over the world, not to mention the President and First Lady. This was a first for me. I was attending an intimate dinner with wealthy and powerful people. I was relieved I wasn't asked to sit at the children's table.

President Reagan and I hit it off the moment we met. He was an incredible storyteller - even the Democrats laughed at his jokes. The President and I started to swap jokes. He began with a story that he had heard about a Russian.

A guy goes to buy a car in Russia and the salesman tells him to come back in twenty years. The guy asks, "Should I come back in the morning or in the afternoon?"

The salesman says, “What’s the difference? It’s twenty years from now.”

The guy replies, “The plumber is coming that morning.”

Everyone at the table cracked up. Now it was my turn. I knew that if I wasn’t funny, I’d never work this country again. I took a deep breath and said, “When the Americans landed on the moon, it was a huge blow to the pride of the Russian Premier, Brezhnev. So he called all the Russian scientists into his office and said, ‘The Americans landed on the moon, so we have to land on the sun.’ The scientists said, ‘Mr. President, we can’t do it. We will burn up.’ Brezhnev answered, ‘Do you think I’m stupid? You will land at night.’” Everybody laughed and our joke exchange continued throughout the night.

President Reagan still holds the record for being the oldest person ever to become the Commander-in-Chief. He told me, “You don’t stop laughing because you grow old - you grow old because you stop laughing.” Years later as the former President suffered from the devastating effects of Alzheimer’s, his family reported he has never lost his sense of humor.

That night as we were laughing around the dinner table the tension in the world was escalating. The Cold War was at the height of its "sniffles" and threatened to break out into a full-blown sneezing fit at any moment. There were many trouble spots in the world. That very night President Reagan had to send helicopters to Libya to deal with Colonel Khadafi. Standing behind President Reagan the entire night was a marine in full dress uniform. Handcuffed to his wrist he had a briefcase (called the "football," of all things) containing the nuclear codes. I was sitting at the dinner table with the man who had the power to launch a nuclear attack that could lead to the destruction of the entire world. When he bombed it was totally different than when I bombed. Still, I chose my jokes carefully that night. I must have made a good impression on the President because I got a call a few months later to perform for him and the most senior members of his administration. When I told my mother about performing in front of President Reagan's cabinet, she said, "Great, I'd like to go with you. I've always wanted to see Nancy's china."

During the time that I got to know President Reagan, America and Russia were building up their nuclear weapons based on the theory that "the one with the biggest rocket wins." This nuclear race was called M.A.D., appropriate acronym for Mutually Assured Destruction. In other words, "If you're gonna blow us up, we're gonna blow you up, too." Looking back, M.A.D. could've also stood for Miraculously Avoided Death. The U.S. and Soviet Union were like two ridiculously oversized school kids taunting each other on the playground, but with much more at stake than who would win an arm-wrestling match.

Every year diplomats from America and the U.S.S.R. would sit down and try and come up with a solution to the arms race. These annual U.S./U.S.S.R. summits were supposed to be an opportunity to find a solution. Since both the U.S. and the U.S.S.R. had vastly different political ideologies, the two diplomats would sit in a room for days and not even speak with each other. It was like they had been married for forty-five years. Very little progress was ever made at these meetings until 1985 when Mikhail Gorbachev took over as the leader of the U.S.S.R. Gorbachev was the guy with the birthmark on his head in the shape of Poland, but he had a lot more than that to offer. Now suddenly both countries had leaders who were open-minded and charismatic.

Then President Reagan had the wild idea of going over to Russia to meet with Gorbachev and he wanted to tell some jokes during a speech he was scheduled to give at the University of Moscow, to loosen up the audience of stiff Russian politicians. So I got a call from the White House chief speechwriter, who asked me to help with Reagan's speech. I was flabbergasted. Me? Write speeches? Even Charo made fun of my English.

So just like that, I became a comedy writer for the President of the United States. Usually it's the other way around - the President supplies the comedy to the writers, but this President wanted to make sure that the jokes in his speech were palatable for the Russian audience. He was sure that humor was a great way to connect with the Russians. As for me, I was sure that if my jokes didn't go over well I would be exiled from both countries. This worried me immensely because I didn't want to be the official comedian for Fidel Castro.

President Reagan and Mr. Gorbachev met at the Moscow summit and, fortunately, Gorbachev showed he possessed a sense of humor, too. It was the first time anyone can recall seeing a Russian and American leader sitting in the same room smiling.

That summit turned out to be the most successful in history. There were landmark treaties and military agreements forged that marked the beginning of the end of the Cold War. Finally, it seemed, they had stopped going "M.A.D." Years later I heard a story of how the summit had nearly collapsed. After several days of negotiating, Reagan and Gorbachev weren't making any progress. At one point Reagan got up and headed for the door. Then he stopped, turned around with a big smile on his face, extended his hand to Gorbachev and said, "Let's start over. My name is Ronnie. Can I call you Misha?" Gorbachev smiled back and that was the end of the Berlin Wall.

I remember sitting in front of the television at my home in Hollywood watching President Reagan deliver the speech that I had helped to write. He started with one of the jokes I had written. "I hear they've been having problems in Russia getting rid of the old regime that's been sitting around for years," Reagan said. "I also understand that there's an old Russian fable that when a baby is born, an angel comes down and kisses the child. If the child gets kissed on the forehead, he becomes an incredible thinker. If he gets kissed on the lips, he becomes an incredible speaker. If he's kissed on the hand, he becomes an artist. Now, I don't know where the angel kissed these people who have been sitting there for so many years..." After he delivered the punch line, there was utter silence. My heart sank and my first thought was, "I'd better give Fidel a call." Then I realized that the audience of Russian politicians didn't speak English and had to wait for the translation. A moment later, when the translator was finished, there was a huge laugh from the crowd and an even bigger sigh of relief from my couch.

Like my engineer friend, I had helped to build a bridge over a raging river of uncertainty - a bridge between the two most powerful nations in the world. Like my doctor friend, I had helped, in a small way, to heal some wounds - the old antagonisms that stopped the superpowers from making the progress that the whole world desperately needed. Like a teacher, I had watched a new relationship grow and develop. It was especially sweet to me that that relationship was between my old country and my new one.

I am a court jester and proud of it. They might not build a statue honoring me, but then again, I'll never have to duck after telling a joke to the President. Hopefully, the only "killing" that anyone will experience as a result of one of my jokes is dying by laughter.

A Shot of Smirnoff

The clerk said "All of my fish were raised on farms and would perish in the wild." My daughter thought the idea of fish growing up on farms with pigs and cows was pretty funny.

Chapter 24

The Best Christmas I Ever Spent Was with a Mexican Turtle

It was Christmas of 1999 and my wife and I had been separated for a while. I had decided to take my children to Cancun, Mexico, so we could spend a traditional family Christmas season together. To me, "I'm dreaming of a white Christmas" means the scalding white beaches of Cancun.

We woke up on the morning of Christmas Eve and my children wanted to know if we were going to have a Christmas tree. I told them that evergreens weren't often found on postcards representing the Mexican landscape, so I thought we'd be out of luck on finding a Christmas tree. I was racking my brain trying to think of a way to teach my children the true meaning of Christmas in this non-traditional setting. I told them that Christmas was a time to be thankful for what you already have and that it should be more about giving than getting.

For years my wife and I had practiced an unusual variation on the tradition of gift giving on holidays and birthdays. On our own birthdays, rather than receive gifts, we would instead give gifts to our loved ones. Since we didn't know anyone in Mexico, finding someone to give a gift to was going to be a challenge. Then it hit me - perhaps the receiver of the gift didn't have to be a person. I gathered my two children around and told them we were going to go to the pet store and buy a fish and release it back into the ocean.

My daughter looked at me and said, "Why would we want to do that?"

I told her that we were going to give the fish the gift of freedom and that it would be much happier swimming in the ocean.

"Yeah, until he gets eaten by a bigger fish," Natasha said. My daughter's knowledge of the food chain momentarily put a damper on my spirits, but it was Christmas and I decided to forge ahead.

I flagged down a cab driver that spoke a little English and asked him to take us to a place where we could find some fish. He took us to the ocean. After some creative gesturing I was finally able to communicate to him that we were looking for a pet store. Since it was Christmas Eve, this took a bit of doing, but we finally found a shop that was open. I asked the cabby to wait for us outside while we went in.

Pet stores in America usually smell like a combination of dogs and cats, guinea pigs and exotic birds. Mexican pet stores factor in the bonus round amenities of high heat and lack of air conditioning to provide an authentic animal aroma. We looked around and asked the owner if any of his fish could be released into the ocean. He couldn't understand why we would want to spend money on a pet and then throw it away. Then he said that all of his fish were raised on farms and would perish in the wild. My daughter thought the idea of fish growing up on farms with pigs and cows was pretty funny, but I explained to her it wasn't quite like that.

After searching through the five pet stores that were open on Christmas Eve, my daughter was getting more and more annoyed. She finally let out an intentional sigh and said, "If you want to set something free, why don't you just let me go back to the hotel."

My son and the storeowner laughed while I looked over the rest of the animals in the last store. I spied some turtles and inquired what kind they were. The storeowner said they were fresh water turtles and were caught in the wild. He told me there was a lagoon on the golf course nearby and that the turtle would no doubt survive if we decided to let it go there.

I was still concerned about taking a chance with this turtle's life. I gently picked her up. With one swift breaststroke her nails tore into my flesh so quickly that I instinctively dropped her on the floor. Without missing a beat, she ran under the counter. My kids broke out in laughter and I was convinced that this turtle could survive living in New York, let alone a golf course pond.

So I decided that we would purchase a turtle and let it

go in the wild. Well it wasn't really the "wild," since the lagoon was on a golf course in a posh country club setting. I told my kids that we were going to give the turtle her freedom. We got back into the cab and, since it was getting dark, we headed to the hotel.

We didn't have time to put the turtle into the lagoon that night so she spent Christmas Eve with us in the hotel room. The turtle was quite happy staying in the bathtub in a few inches of water. We fed her some fish we brought back from the restaurant.

When we woke up it was a beautiful, sunny morning in this resort city. Soon we were walking down the street, my daughter, my son and a turtle that had just spent the night in a nice hotel. We received some odd looks from passersby as we strolled to our destination. I am sure they thought we were the Russian-American version of the Addams Family.

We finally got to the golf course and found that a chain-link fence protected its entire perimeter. I knew we couldn't just walk on the course, even though technically we were a foursome. By this time my children had grown to like the idea of setting the turtle free and were disappointed to think we might not get to the lagoon. We walked a little further down the road and found a gate. A sign hung from the rusty chain-link that read, "No Trespassing." I thought for a second that teaching my children the lesson of giving while trespassing might send a mixed message, but quite frankly, the turtle was getting heavy.

I forced the gate open and we all ducked into the bushes on the edge of the third fairway. My kids spotted a good-sized lagoon that was about a nine-iron from where we stood. There was nobody on the fairway so we walked toward the turtle's new home. Being quite a miserable golfer in my previous attempts at the game, this was by far the most fun I'd ever had on a golf course.

My children took the turtle and slowly lowered her into the murky water at the edge of the lagoon. The stunned turtle floated there for a few seconds before realizing she was free. She gave us one last look and we all thought she had a smile on her face. Then with a flick of her tail, she took off like a shot.

"I hope you like your freedom, Mrs. Turtle," my son said.

My daughter wondered out loud, "Hope she likes her home here. Maybe she'll find a husband and have babies."

My son added, "Yeah, maybe she'll build a house in the swamp."

I saw my children's faces light up as they watched the

turtle disappear into the muck and I realized that giving this turtle its freedom probably meant more to me than it did to the turtle.

We walked back to the hotel and I noticed there was a skip in everyone's step. Alexander asked, "What do you think she's doing now?"

"Bet she's having a nap," Natasha answered.

They both looked at me for my answer. "I don't know what she's doing, but I know she's happy."

We arrived back at the hotel and enjoyed a traditional Christmas meal of tacos, black beans and turtle soup. It was one of the best Christmases we've ever had.

Now when I look back on that unusual holiday celebration, it's obvious to me that the lesson I was teaching my children wasn't just the joy of giving. The long trek to the lagoon, the fence that tried to keep us out and the beautiful new home for the turtle were all metaphors for my own journey to the United States.

My children are too young to understand what it was like for me to grow up in communist Russia, but when the time comes and they are curious about why their father chose to leave his own country to pursue a dream that required freedom, I think I'll give the answer by starting with a question.

"Remember the turtle we set free in Mexico?"

A Shot of Smirnoff

Our neighbors brought us over our first real American breakfast: English muffins, French toast and Canadian bacon. We had traded communism for cholesterol, but we were happy to make that swap. I thought, so this is what it must feel like to be an American?

Chapter 25

The Real Sweet Lady Liberty

Our family came to America seeking a new home and a better life, but God delivered miracles to us through the kindness of strangers.

For many years we had heard so much about the Statue of Liberty. Seeing her as our airliner approached New York City reminded us that we had achieved the first part of our dream - arriving safely in America. Now we could work on the second part of our American dream - learning Spanish.

Our dream was to be free. Free to live the life we chose, not the life that was chosen for us. Arriving in the United States was the beginning, but we needed to make our own way with very little money and almost no possessions. About the only thing we possessed was a genuine will to succeed in America, although we were as frightened as we were excited about our new life here.

The first encouraging sign greeted us as we stepped off the airplane in New York. Actually, it was more than a sign, it was a giant billboard with the slogan "America Loves Smirnoff" emblazoned across it, and I didn't even think anybody knew we were coming!

Through an interpreter, a customs officer asked me what I planned to do in America. When I told him that I wanted to become a famous comedian, he laughed hysterically. I thought I was off to a pretty good start. Then I saw a dog sniffing our luggage. I asked the interpreter what was going on and he said, "The dogs are looking for drugs."

I said, "I heard in America people are hooked on drugs, but dogs?"

The customs officer laughed even louder. At that point I realized it was going to be a lot easier to make Americans laugh than I had thought.

The first order of business in our new country was to find a place to live. I was thrilled with the idea of finally having our own family apartment.

It's hard to believe now, but for 26 years I shared a bedroom with my parents. It sounds like a strange situation and it was. When I was a little boy and my parents wanted to be intimate, my father would tell me to go look out the window. One time he asked me, "What do you see, Yakov?"

I said, "Our neighbors being intimate."

He said, "How can you tell?"

"Because their son is looking at me!"

Needless to say, finding a nice apartment with at least two bedrooms was a top priority for all of us.

Most of the apartment managers in New York spoke Spanish. Since we only spoke Russian, the search for a new home wasn't that easy. When I asked if any apartments were available, I'd often hear, "No comprende!" Naturally, I thought this meant "no apartment."

Having quickly figured this out, I began asking, "Comprende?" When a manager said, "Si," I thought, great apartment "C" is available! After carrying our stuff up and down the three flights of stairs I realized my Spanish was as bad as my English.

Finally, after much searching, we found a tiny apartment that was vacant. The rent was $240 a month, but we only had $50 between us. It was then that I first experienced the extraordinary kindness of Americans.

The building manager was a gentle 79 year-old woman with a cherubic smile. Her name was Mrs. Landau. She saw how tired and afraid we were and did something I'll never forget. She let us have that apartment, even though we didn't have the money to pay for it. Later, I found out that Mrs. Landau paid the difference out of her own pocket that first month, even though she barely had enough money for herself. She gave us our first home in America.

When I found out that she had covered our shortfall, I asked her, "Why did you do that?"

She smiled and said, "Eighty years ago, my parents came to America. They had nothing, yet someone helped them get started. I guess that's what we do here, we help others less fortunate than ourselves."

On our first night in our apartment we slept on the floor. It was the most comforting sleep I had had since leaving Russia. Early the next morning, my father was sitting on a suitcase looking at the New York skyline. The city was just waking up when he said to me, "Yakov, look out the window." Immediately, from across the room, I heard my mother say, "Not now - I have a headache!"

We stared out at the morning sky together. I looked over at my mother who was crying. I asked her what was wrong and she said, "We don't have anything here. We don't have furniture, we don't even have anything to sleep on."

My father and I were trying to comfort her when there was a knock at the door. At first we were afraid it might be the KGB or even worse, an Avon lady.

I opened the door cautiously and what I saw filled my heart with joy. There was Mrs. Landau, with a big smile that seemed to stretch from one side of her sweet little face to the other. Behind her, stretching all the way along the hallway and disappearing down the staircase, was a line of people carrying things, everything from dishes and blankets to clothing and food. My first thought was, "These people are so poor they're carrying around all of their belongings. At least we have an apartment!"

Mrs. Landau looked up at me and said, "I'd like you to meet your neighbors." One by one, these strangers filed into our apartment to give us the things we so desperately needed. Some greeted us, some just smiled, but their kindness spoke in every language - "Welcome home."

Our new neighbors even gave us things we'd never seen before. My mother used a waffle iron for the first time and ruined two pairs of my pants.

After our new neighbors left, we sat in silence with tears in our eyes. I thought, 'so this is what it must feel like to be an American.' My mother cried again, but this time the tears that ran down her cheeks were tears of joy.

The following morning, the woman next door brought us over our first real American breakfast: English muffins, French toast and Canadian bacon. We had traded communism for cholesterol, but we were happy to make that swap. I realized that the essence of America was that everybody was welcome. We were welcomed with kindness and acceptance and that made us want to treat others the same way.

We have been living in the United States for more than 20 wonderful years now. During my time here I have seen so many things that confirm what I had always thought about as a little boy in Russia - that America is the land of freedom, kindness and compassion, but since I came to America, a lot of people told me how America is not as kind as it was and how people don't care for one another anymore. I don't personally believe it's true. I think perhaps we learn how to look at negative things.

In Russia, 270 million people believed in communism because the government would not let us see anything else, but in America, we have a choice. We can see what we want to see, we just have to want to see it. I believe that we see what we seek. If we seek something bad, it's easy to find - just turn on the Jerry Springer show, but we have freedom here - we have freedom to choose. We can choose to look at police corruption or we can choose to see the police officer that uses his lunch hour to go and donate blood. We can focus on the sorrow of high school shootings or we can see the Little League baseball coach who says to his kids, "Don't worry, you may be small, but you're slow." Yet he hosts a large pizza party for the whole team out of his own pocket after every game, win or lose.

We can focus on the shocking kidnapping of a child or see the inner strength of dozens of people who fan out through frozen fields, trudging through the snow day and night looking for that little girl they have never met, but love as much as they love their own daughter or granddaughter who is safe at home. We can choose to watch the footage of airplanes crashing into the World Trade Center over and over again or we can see the courage of a young mother who, fighting back her tears, tells her 5 year-old son that there was an accident in Daddy's building and he's gone, but because he worked so high up, God took him straight to heaven.

It's not easy to find good in tragedy, but I believe the human spirit is not measured by the size of an act but by the size of the heart. Just like those brave men and women in New York, tirelessly looking through the rubble day and night for some signs of life, it's up to you and me to dig down deep and find the good. It's not gone, it's just buried under tons of grief and despair.

It's up to you and me to see those everyday heroes and never take them for granted. I know from first-hand experience that the world is full of wonderful individuals, just waiting to be discovered by those who have eyes to see. They come in all different shapes and sizes, from that sweet angel, Mrs. Landau, to the person you see in the grocery store or at work. Every day, in every small town or big city, Americans say, "We care" in the silent ways that speak louder than any act of terrorism ever could. Do you know why? Because you speak with your hearts! Our neighbor, Mrs. Landau, did not speak Russian, yet her heart told me everything I needed to know about this country and though she had to stand on the tip of her toes to reach five feet in height, to me she stood every inch as tall as sweet Lady Liberty.

Acknowledgements

I'd like to begin by thanking three guys who started everything off. Buzz Nutley (his name is almost as good as mine) is a hilarious comedian who does stand-up around the country. His combination of sensitivity and humor struck a chord with me and I asked him to help draw these stories out of me. He not only drew them out of me, he gave me a creative enema! But he sacrificed a lot in the process. Even though his regular diet is Big Macs and Coca-Cola, he spent two weeks with me going to juice bars and drinking wheat grass as we mined the raw material for this book.

Will Wilkinson's a truly spiritual person who has a strong left-brain sense of structure. He brought a stability and rationality to the process of writing a book with a lot of crazy comedians. However, while Will may have been the zookeeper, he did occasionally act like one of the monkeys!

Michael Mandrick is the tallest of all the contributors.

The final touches could only have been seen at his height. His sensitivity matched well with my sense of humor.

Bruce Clark is the comedy writer who pulled the whole project together and put the finishing touches on the first final draft. A Hollywood Agent introduced Bruce to me. I had asked him if he knew of a comedy writer who could punch it up a little more. “Yakov, with this book you’re gonna be known as the Russian Mark Twain,” he told me. “But even Mark Twain could use a few more jokes.” Then he pointed me toward Bruce Clark.

Of course, like all comedy, this book has gone through a hundred different revisions since that Pulitzer worthy first draft. Two people I want to mention particularly are Brian Scully, another great writer who helped me find the right words to express my emotions and feelings and Victoria St. George, the “closer.” Vicki may not be as funny as the others who worked on this, but she has a good sense of the ridiculous and a “can-do” attitude. With Vicki’s help, the final draft of this book was produced in record time (record for me, that is). The final touches were made by Maren Schmidt who is a dear friend and former principle of my children’s school. She graded my paper after she had finished grading all the kids’ homework. So if there are any mistakes it is her fault.

I have been fortunate in my life to have many people encourage and help me every step of the way. Marcy Sheimoff is a good friend who has written several of the *Chicken Soup for the Soul* books. She helped by urging me to write this book and she has given me great suggestions on content, stories and ideas. Mike Rydell and Joe Maderas are both old friends and great comedy writers who have honed their craft at places like *The Tonight Show*. They have given me amazing advice and quite a few jokes that found their way into this book. Towards the end of the process, Honey Scott, my personal assistant, typed and retyped a lot of the stories. I could tell by the look on her face whether she approved or disapproved of what she was typing and her taste helped me to shape this book.

A special thanks goes to Tad Schinke who has been my life coach for several years. Tad sees the greatness in me and helps me refine it. He grounds me, helps me look at things from a different perspective and encourages me along the way.

Others whom I may or may not have mentioned in this book, but who have had a huge impact on my life, include Mitzy Shore, the owner of The Comedy Store, Ronald and Nancy Reagan, who have set examples throughout their incredible lives, comedians like Jerry Sienfeld, Bill Cosby,

Robin Williams, David Letterman (I would never be who I am without your Top Ten list), Johnny Carson, Regis Philbin and Jay Leno. I'd like to thank Brooke Shields for helping me learn about hummus and my ex-wife, Linda, who is my great friend and my partner in raising our two incredible kids. Special thanks go to Denny Hilton, a good friend who makes me laugh, and Gary Powell, whom you'll meet in the pages of this book. I also want to thank Terri Tucker, who encouraged me to become stronger and face the challenges of my life, and Kathy Werner, nanny of my kids and also a great friend and sounding board. She helps me understand the philosophies I have studied and practice them daily.

I have always sought out great teachers in hopes of learning life's lessons. Why take the hits yourself if someone has already been around the boxing ring? Some of my teachers include Tony Robbins, Stephen Covey, Deepak Chopra, Pat Allen, David Deida, Neal David Walsh and Neal Clark Warren. They have helped me grow both as a man and as a comedian. Luckily, I'm still funnier than any of them!

I must give special thanks to the incredible staff of my theatre in Branson. They make working there a lot of fun. You're lucky when you're at work and can't wait to go home and lucky when you're at home and you can't wait to go to work. On both counts, I consider myself a very lucky man.

I am thankful to my source, my motivation, the heart of my comedy and my audience. To all the people who ever laughed at my jokes or were touched by my emotions, thank you for coming. It would be a lot harder to do it without you. Thanks for receiving my humor and giving back your laughter.

I hope as you read this book you'll see where I get a lot of my inspiration. I continue to be inspired by my mom. I'm happy that Mom stuck around long enough to see my transformation into a full-functioning adult. Her wisdom in her golden years have helped her to not only understand my transformation, but to also transform herself. I especially want to mention my children Natasha and Alexander, whom I love with the deepest meaning of the word. They are helping me become a better person every day because I want to lead them by example. Their wisdom and laughter fill a tender spot in my heart and keep me young. They are a constant source of joy, wonder and humor. I was in California on business and wanted to visit Disneyland. I missed my kids and I called them as I entered the park. I said, "Kids I am in the happiest place on earth." They said, "Dad, are you at Pizza Hut."